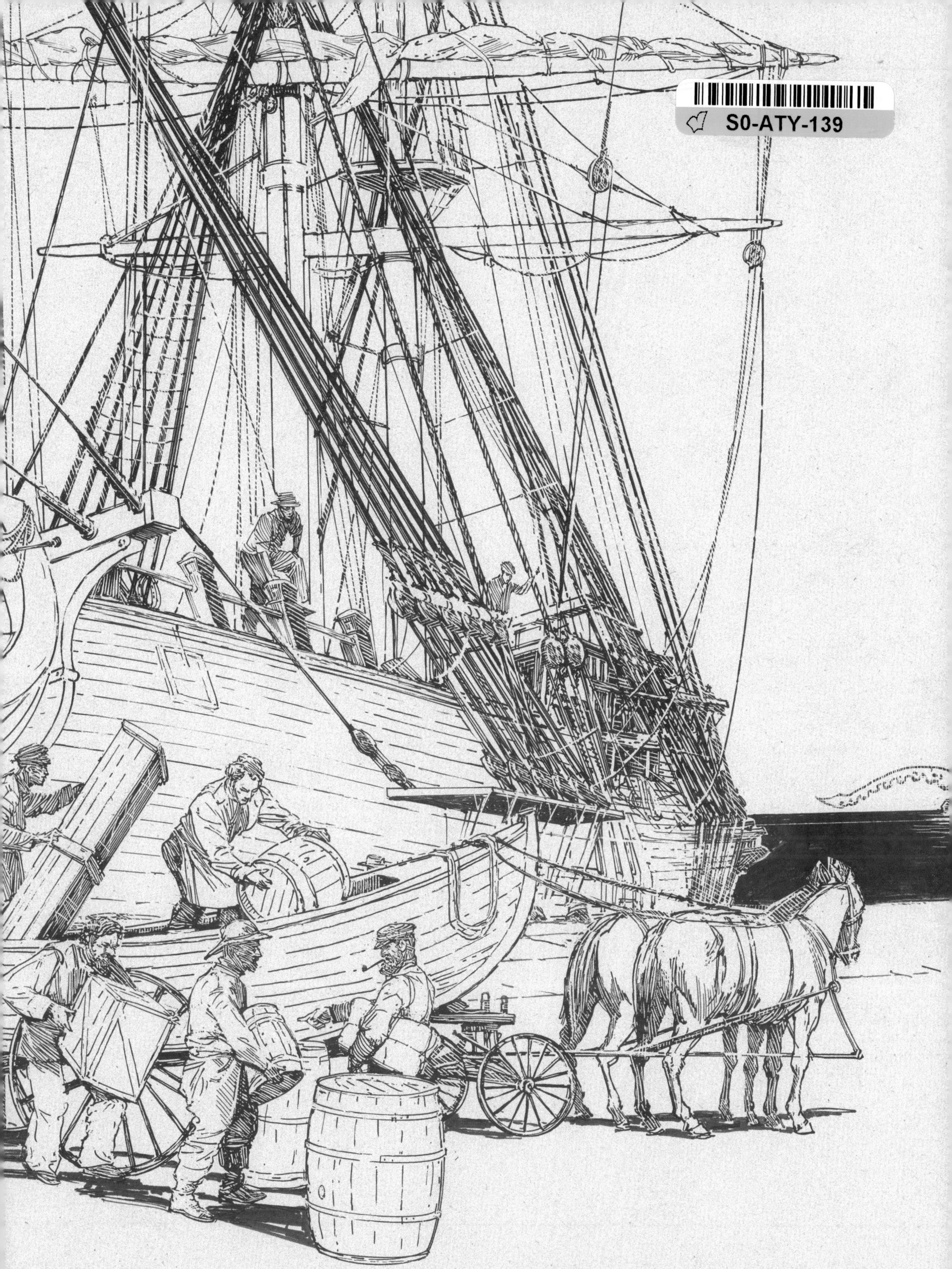

Twenty-Thousand Leagues Under the Sea

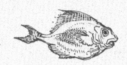

Design and color: Jim & Ruth Keegan
Color assist: Alex Wald
Publisher and editor: John Fleskes
Scanning assist: Cliff Moore, and James Walker II.

First Printing
January 2009

Hardbound Edition ISBN: 978-1-933865-08-9
Hardbound Deluxe Edition ISBN: 978-1-933865-09-6

Flesk Publications™
P.O. Box 3174
Santa Cruz, CA 95063
www.fleskpublications.com
info@fleskpublications.com

JULES VERNE'S
TWENTY-THOUSAND LEAGUES UNDER THE SEA

ILLUSTRATED BY
GARY GIANNI

COLORS BY JIM & RUTH KEEGAN

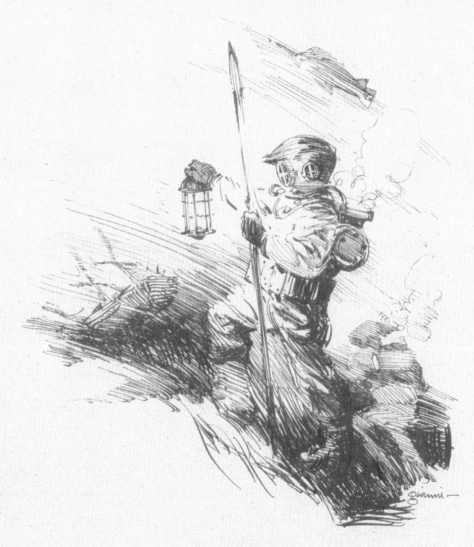

FLESK

THE ARDENT BLASPHEMERS

BY RAY BRADBURY

CONSIDER AMERICA, first of all the new breed of nations.

Consider America, a nation, because of its newness, ardent in its blasphemy.

Set in motion by the centrifuge of the great wheel of the Industrial Revolution, this people flung themselves across sea prairies to stand on New England rim-rock and fling themselves yet on across land prairies. Shocking other ages, they blasphemed down the meadows and over hills as ancient as the memory of Jerusalem.

Consider America, her fire-dragon locomotives huffing out vast devil bursts of fluming spark, setting the lion-grass afire as they went.

Come to a forest, cut it down. Come to a mountain, quarry it to pebbles. Skip the pebbles across God's lakes. Build *new* mountains, finally, upright, and ornamented with man's prideful encrustations. Then run men up and down elevator shafts to a heaven no longer believed in from a hell much better ignored.

Consider the authors who lived in and with these men and wrote to channel this blasphemy, express it in symbols about which such men could enthuse like devil children. With a new nation being dreamt to life, set to rights with fabulous new toys, the uneasy dreamers cast about and came up with two most ardent blasphemers:

Herman Melville.

Jules Verne.

"American" authors, both.

Melville, the New Englander, and Verne, the Frenchman, you say, Americans both?

"American" yes in their newness and their attack upon the universe and this world rolling through that universe.

Another nation could have been "American" first. The seeds of man's mechanical reaction to Nature were cast forth first in England and France. But the flowering of what other ages might have considered an insidious tree was in this raw nation under God which would soon ask Him to move over, jump aside, step down. We might not even ask His pardon while we scourged the mineral gut, packed once-holy echoes in electronic boxes to deal them forth commercially, split atoms as handily as peas, and dared God to answer back in equal thunders.

I say, another nation could have done this. But the accidents of time and circumstance dubbed us unholy first. Others follow us in our sacrilege: the Japanese and his insect-clicking camera, the Frenchman flung about by our L.P. jive, the Italian hopping Rome's hills on angry adaptations of our motorbikes.

The sacrilege was inevitable.

Once set the wheel invented by some fine fool of a first blasphemer in motion just beyond old Egypt and it rolls up in the late '80s of our time such dust clouds as would dim the bright visage of any spoiled God. Wheels within wheels within wheels rolled forth upon our land and, later, way in the middle of our outraged God's air.

And being firstest with the mostest, we not only *did* but *read*, and having read did *more*.

And Jules Verne was our text and testament, followed close by packs of "evil" boys like Tom Swift and his Flying Machine plus his A.C.-D.C. I.B.M Powered-Circuited Grandmother.

I Sing the Body Electric! Cried Whitman.

And Americans wound tight their robot devices and set them free to gnaw ugliness across the territories which now, very late, we must clean up after.

But let us go back to our literary beginnings.

Why, in introducing you to this book by Jules Verne, do I summon forth the lunar name of Herman Melville? What relation do I see between a Frenchman benevolent as a good uncle in his eccentricities, and strange cousin Herman who some thought best kept in America's attic?

From the viewpoint of Gothic times peering ahead at the tidal wave of the future, let me set up these two men.

God, after all, was in His heaven a long while, and things went well for Him, if not His children, upon earth. Those born-but-to-die inhabited His churches and if they questioned, questions were best kept mum in one's mouth or like gum behind the ear.

But send these God-doting children free from Europe, strew and scrabble them across a whole continental surprise, hand them commotions and contraptions of steam and whiffling iron and they pant up frenzies of revenge against God for having maltreated them down the eons.

Out of questions suddenly posed and needs suddenly found most needful, as the steam blew off and the proud dust settled we found:

Mad Captain Ahab.

Mad Captain Nemo.

Moby Dick, the great White Whale.

Nautilus, the whale-seeming submarine, first of its hidden and terrific sort, soaring through sea-meadows amongst sinner sharks and true leviathans.

Look how these two "evil" men implement their "blasphemy."

"Call me Ishmael."

So Melville strikes forth on his search for Moby Dick. In his first chapter we find:

"...Why upon your first voyage as a passenger, did you yourself feel such a mystical vibration, when first told that you and your ship were now out of sight of land? Why did the old Persians hold the sea holy? Why did the Greeks give it a separate deity, and own brother of Jove? Surely all this is not without meaning. And still deeper the meaning of that story of Narcissus, who because he could not grasp the tormenting, mild image he saw in the fountain, plunged into it and was drowned. But that same image, we ourselves see in all rivers and oceans. It is the image of the ungraspable phantom of life; and this is the key to it all."

Why does Ishmael go to sea?

"...Chief among these motives was the overwhelming idea of the great whale himself. Such a portentous and mysterious monster roused all my curiosity. Then the wild and distant seas where he rolled his island bulk; the undeliverable, nameless perils of the whale; these, with all the attending marvels of a thousand Patagonian sights and sounds, helped to sway me to my wish... by reason of these things, then, the whaling voyage was welcome; the great flood-gates of the wonder-world swung open, and in the wild conceits that swayed me to my purpose, two and two there floated into my inmost soul, endless processions of the whale, and, mid most of them all, one grand hooded phantom, like a snow hill in the air."

In *Twenty Thousand Leagues Under the Sea*, Jules Verne starts thus:

"The year 1866 was marked by a strange event, an unexplainable occurrence which is undoubtedly still fresh in everyone's memory.... Several ships had recently met at sea 'an enormous thing,' a long slender object which was sometimes phosphorescent and which was infinitely larger and faster than a whale."

Verne continues:

"The facts concerning this apparition...agreed closely with one another as to the structure of the object or creature in question, the incredible speed of its movements, the surprising power of its locomotion and the strange life with which it seemed endowed. If it was a member of the whale family, it was larger than any so far classified by scientists.... But it did exist—there was no denying this fact any longer—and considering the natural inclination of the human brain toward objects of wonder, one can understand the excitement produced throughout the world by this supernatural apparition."

So two books begin. Both set somewhat the same tone, both strike chords that might recur within the framework of the book to follow. Yet swiftly we perceive rank differences. We soon know that while Uncle Jules is mostly gently mad, cousin Herman is beyond the pale.

We set sail with Ishmael who, unknowing, is in the clutches of wild Ahab, seeking some universal truth shaped to a monster all frightful white named Moby Dick.

We set sail almost simultaneously with Professor Aronnax and Ned Land and Conseil on the *Abraham Lincoln* in search of this other mystery which "in every big city...became the fashion: it was sung in cafés, derided in newspapers and discussed on the stage. Scandal sheets had a marvelous opportunity to print all kinds of wild stories. Even ordinary newspapers—always short of copy—printed articles about every huge, imaginary monster one could think of, from the white whale, the terrible 'Moby Dick' of the far north, to the legendary Norse kraken...."

So we suspect that Uncle Jules has touched minds somewhere down the line with Cousin Herman.

But without any real exchange or superblending of madness. Mr. Verne will go his own way with his "educated" vengeance, leaving Melville with his Shakespearean terrors and laments.

We do not meet Moby Dick face to face, we only have Ahab's leg torn off in retrospect, until very late in Melville.

But Verne, in Chapter VI of *Twenty Thousand Leagues*, hoves his "monster" to view and swallows our Jonahs whole and entire.

Thus ending the tale as Melville might end it?

No, thus starting to show us the vast differences between the odd American-type French writer and the truly driven New England author-sailor soon to be despairing customs inspector.

Let us compare some few quotes from each writer.

Here are some from *Moby Dick*:

"His three boats stove around him, and oars and men both whirling in the eddies; one captain, seizing the line-knife from his broken prow, had dashed at the Whale.... That Captain was Ahab.... And then it was, that suddenly sweeping his sickle-shaped lower jaw beneath him, Moby Dick had reaped away Ahab's leg, as a mower a blade of grass in the field. No turbaned Turk, no hired Venetian or Malay, could have smote him with more seeming malice... ever since that almost fatal encounter, Ahab had cherished a wild vindictiveness against the whale, all the more fell for that in his frantic morbidness he at last came to identify with him, not only all his bodily woes, but all his intellectual and spiritual exasperations. The White Whale swam before him as the monomaniac incarnation of all those malicious agencies which some deep men feel eating them, till they are left living on with half a heart and half a lung.... All that most maddens and torments; all that stirs up the lees of things; all truth with malice in it; all that cracks the sinews and cakes the brain; all the subtle demonisms of life and thought; all evil, to crazy Ahab, were visibly personified, and made practically assailable in Moby Dick. He piled upon the whale's white hump the sum of

all the general rage and hate felt by his whole race from Adam down; and then, as if his chest had been a mortar, he burst his hot heart's shell upon it."

Also, Ahab, speaking to Starbuck:

"Hark ye yet again,—the little lower layer. All visible objects, man, are but as pasteboard masks. But in each event—in the living act, the undoubted deed—there, some unknown but still reasoning thing puts forth the mouldings of its features from behind the unreasoning mask. If man will strike, strike through the mask! How can the prisoner reach outside except by thrusting through the wall? To me, the white whale is that wall, shoved near to me. Sometimes I think there's naught beyond. But 'tis enough. He tasks me; he heaps me; I see in him outrageous strength, with an inscrutable malice sinewing it. That inscrutable thing is chiefly what I hate; and be the white whale agent, or be the white whale principal, I will wreak that hate upon him. Talk not to me of blasphemy, man: I'd strike the sun if it insulted me."

Compare the above with these quotes from Verne's somewhat more differently "touched" Nemo:

"Professor...I'm not what you would call a civilized man! I've broken with all society for reasons which I alone can appreciate. I therefore don't obey its rules, and I advise you never to refer to them again in front of me!"

Aronnax asks Nemo:

"You love the sea, don't you, Captain?"

"Yes, I love it! The sea is everything. It covers seven-tenths of the globe. Its breath is pure and healthy. It is an immense desert where a man is never alone, for he can feel life quivering all about him. The sea is only a receptacle for all the prodigious, supernatural things that exist inside it; it is only movement and love; it is the living infinite, as one of your poets has said. And in fact, Professor, it contains the three kingdoms of nature—mineral, vegetable, and animal. This last is well represented by the four groups of zoophytes, by the three classes of articulata, by the five classes of mollusks, by the three classes of vertebrates, mammals and reptiles, and by those innumerable legions of fish, that infinite order of animals which includes more than thirteen thousand species, only one-tenth of which live in fresh water. The sea is a vast reservoir of nature. The world, so to speak, began with the sea, and who knows but that it will also end in the sea! There lies supreme tranquility. The sea does not belong to tyrants. On its surface, they can still exercise their iniquitous rights, fighting, destroying one another and indulging in their other earthly horrors. But thirty feet below its surface their power ceases, their influence dies out and their domination disappears! Ah, Monsieur, one must live—live within the ocean! Only there can one be independent! Only there do I have no masters! There I am free!"

How different from Melville's:

"When beholding the tranquil beauty and brilliancy of the ocean's skin, one forgets the tiger heart that pants beneath it; and would not willingly remember that this velvet paw but conceals a remorseless fang."

And, in a tranquil, golden moment, Starbuck muses:

"Loveliness unfathomable, as ever lover saw in his young bride's eye. Tell me not of thy teeth-tiered sharks, and thy kidnapping cannibal ways. Let faith oust fact; let fancy oust memory; I look deep down and do believe."

But Ahab will have none of it. He rejects what Nemo gladly accepts.

The sea, with all its terror fleshed in beauty, is preferred by Nemo. Here ignorant hunters hunt from hunger. Above, intelligent men, sated at feasts, hunt from needs best not thought on save in nightmares of sadism and wanton destruction.

> *"Professor...I'm not what you would call a civilized man! I've broken with all society for reasons which I alone can appreciate. I therefore don't obey its rules, and I advise you never to refer to them again in front of me!"*
>
> — Captain Nemo

To kill with the teeth is one thing. To kill with the hand, connected to the heart and thinking brain, is quite another.

"Strike through the mask" cries Ahab.

Better than that, Nemo might reply in an imaginary rebuttal, I will *build* behind the mask, I will *inhabit* the white whale.

After a shocked silence, Nemo might continue something like this:

I will create me a symbol of the deep, a manifestation of God's huge wonders, submersible, long-ranging, capably destructive, submissive to my commands, and I will course ocean seas in same, to spread a more personal and therefore more constructive terror in the world. I will not run after Moby Dick. I will rear him whole and entire and live in his belly and be the Mystery, myself.

So, in sum, Nemo skins together and rivets tight the very symbol most feared and whispered of by Ahab's mind and Ahab's crew. Casting aside any doubts, precluding any inhibitions, Nemo intrudes to the monster's marrow, disinhabits mysticism, evicts terrors like so much trash, and proceeds to police the universe beneath, setting it to rights, harvesting its strange crops, be they animal, vegetable, or mineral-gold from sunken fool's ships to be distributed to the world's needy.

In this we find then that Verne is less blasphemous than Melville. He does not so much try to find and kill God in His lounging room as set His miraculous kitchen to percolating in synchronous, perceivable, and therefore serenity-inducing rhythms. Given choices. Melville's Ahab would blow up the Clock Tower. Verne's Nemo would collect the exploded parts, put the whole back better than new and ask the world's citizens to tell their lives by it, be on time for one another from now on.

Verne accepts the natural world and would ask all men to accept its secret ways and join in making themselves over nearer to the hidden heart of this secret so as to utilize it, channel it, reconstruct it where necessary, to give man extra years and vitality.

Melville cannot accept and with Ahab rages at the blind maunderings of a God he cannot comprehend.

Ah, well, says Verne, let us work, let us think, then let us work again until we sweat. We shall win through, or die trying.

No, says Melville, we cannot win. And vainly thrusts the harpoon to deflate the God-symboled Whale.

Verne cares less about killing the symbol, more of rendering the Leviathan out for oil to light the flickerful lamps of a thinking world.

Thinking maddens Ahab.

Thinking only half-maddens Nemo; more often enlivens and solves problems for him and others who inhabit Verne's literary worlds.

Ahab is mad at the God-universe.

Nemo, more practically, is mad at man himself for not using his gift of brains.

Ahab, being irrationally disturbed at the Invisible, can do little.

Nemo, being distressed at God's children, has at least somewhere to start, material to work with, evil and good men to choose among, dirt to be swept out of corners and from under rugs.

Ahab, in trying to search everywhere, finds nothing.

Nemo, content with good beginnings, looks no further than the next man, and scans his face to guess his dream, and if the dream be bad, there is always the ocean depth to live in, gathering yet richer harvests whereby to relieve the oppressed.

So in the long journey through *Moby Dick* we follow Ahab, knighted by the whale who did so by tearing him asunder, and wearing his terrible crown of now self-inflicted thorns, self-appointing himself to a tragic end.

We wonder what Nemo would have thought of all this?

Glancing in from the kitchen where he might be busy serving forth foods to button up men's souls and sluice their veins with revivifying wonder, Nemo might well debate who that demented sea-king was, unnecessarily throwing and dragging himself about the throne room. We could well imagine Nemo hurrying in to offer a bracing hot drink, or finally slapping Ahab once across the face, seizing his shoulders to shake him, at last, and tell him to behave.

Faced with similar cataclysms we know Ahab would go down with his ship, shaking his fists at Fate.

While Nemo would vanish beneath the sea still bailing out water with his cupped hands.

Ahab's ship pursues an unpursuable God, crying out against His characteristically ill behavior.

Nemo's ship pursues men to remind them of their wickedness, to improve it, or be sunk.

Ahab's ship moves most of the time in nightmare.

Nemo's moves in kaleidoscopic wonders, in rainbow beauties of life thrown forth in multitudinous displays. Only man is nightmare, and Nemo has a better dream to give him as anodyne.

Moby Dick rams Ahab's *Pequod* because that ship is the engine of blasphemy, directed at the Mystery.

Nemo's *Nautilus* rams naval ships because they blaspheme against the better and best spirit of humankind.

In the long history of the world, God's motto was writ on man's brow this way:

> Yours not to reason why,
> Yours to be born and die.

So Melville's Whale resents inquiry.

But Verne's *Nautilus* is the machine of curiosity, erasing the above motto, prolonging a searchful blasphemy into construction and jigsawing the grand puzzle into a whole.

Ahab orders God to reform Himself in a better image.

Nemo asks mankind to reform in cleaner, higher-spirited, well-mannered ranks.

Both men, being reformers, inevitably destroy for their purposes.

Ahab takes all with him to the sea-bottom in his Shakespearean frenzy.

Nemo, less mad, like many reformers nevertheless winds up killing men to make them behave. Death instructs people well in peace, and by the time he is done, Nemo has killed just as surely as if his aims had been bad.

The sea closes over both men.

But Ahab dead is doomed just as he was doomed alive.

While hope lives on after Nemo, when, either through remorse or inadvertency, he puts his ship down into the Maelstrom. We are unsure of his death.

On the last page of his book, Verne offers us this thought:

"If [the *Nautilus* has survived] and if Captain Nemo still inhabits the ocean—the country of his adoption—then may the hatred be appeased in his savage heart! May the contemplation of so many wonders extinguish in him the spirit of revenge! May the judge disappear and the scientist continue his peaceful exploration of the seas! However strange his destiny may be, it is also sublime!"

And in that sublimity lies hope for Nemo and his American nephews, the boys who have grown to manhood and machinery since.

For Ahab the hope would be meaningless. If by some miracle Melville's madman should open his cold eyes at the sea-bottom, the contemplation of Verne's rainbow wonders would but drive him deeper into his own abyss. Melville's maelstrom, sucking down through the gorge of Ahab's soul, could swallow Verne's toy *Nautilus* whole.

But swallow it it never will.

For what we have examined here are two ways of looking at the world. Ages alternate with doses of despair and tonics of survival. Some ages balance between. We are given choices. Some ages do not choose, and thus lose ground in the great vote-taking of time and the deliverance of power either into or out of their hands.

One hundred years ago, this Yea-sayer and this Nay-sayer, literarily anyway, offered us the choice of the nodded or the shaken head. Separated by thousands of sea-miles, yet cheek-by-jowl, these authors represented two halves of the newly emergent American attitude toward the world, and debated whether to live under nature's thunderbolts and rainstorms; accept, tolerate, as all had done before.

One decided to give God as good as he got, and stormed heaven as if it were hell.

The other favored pacing God, running at His elbow, recharging man's batteries, using His juice, so as to later circumvent Him with newer, brighter machineries of sacrilege. These devices saved men's lives when God said die, they reared sick men tall whilst God said fall down dead, lie cold.

And now that we are well into this age of electronics and have begun to worry about how to let some new kind of God-concept back in through even so much as a side-door, we shall witness the pendulum swing, quite often, between Ahab and Nemo. On successive days we may feel both tempted to utter destruction or utter mechanical creativity or combinations and variations on both.

If I assay right, we in America are just emerging from a period inclining toward the Melvillean. We are tempted to hurl our sick heart into God's face.

But I think instead we should listen to the good and reassuring beat of the circuiting mechanical pump in our hospitals, where man's salt blood bypasses his failing heart to be aerated and, returned to his waiting and hopeful body. The medical machines of our time, throbbing, would have seemed music to Verne. They calm the ravening intellect that would run too fast to change the world, perhaps by disaster.

The world *will* change, at any rate, through outright fury, neglect, or through the mild but dedicated blasphemy of such as Nemo.

Ahab might explode a hydrogen bomb to shake the foundations of God.

But in the fright-flash of illumination, at some distance, we would see Nemo re-perusing notes made in mathematical symbols to use such energy to send men to the stars rather than scatter them in green milk-glass and radioactive chaff along the shore.

These then are the captains of our American soul. We could choose between them, if we wished, as tomorrow's light comes in the window.

Decide that God has joined the universe with warped and spokeless wheels and so take Melville and invite the Abyss.

Decide that *man's* architecture is in sore need of retrials and testings, and so put in with Mr. Verne.

The latter might be our greatest temptation, for we have always resembled Nemo rather more than Ahab.

We have always been the American Boy Mechanic, his cellar full of home-made helicopters, his attic chocked with canvas batwings, an unfinished rowboat in the basement, a bicycle-built-for-two-hovercraft in the yard.

America was ingenuity. It still is and could be. Spit, string, and tinfoil once our girded armor and the grand dream our goal, we have too often now folded our money into our pockets and strolled off while Doom bided its time and whetted its whistle around the corner.

So surprisingly enough, the book you hold in your hands is more than timely, as are all of Verne's books. Remarkable not so much for what he predicted, and he predicted much—gave bones to boys on which to skin their dreams—but because of its attitude, American in the best sense, that we can somehow make-do somewhere, anywhere, if we collect our spit, save our string, and ball our tinfoil.

Melville wrote to Hawthorne of *Moby Dick*:

"I have written an evil book."

Similarly, seen from other days and ways, Verne might have written some literary friend that yesterday's evil can be hammered into today's good, yesterday's provocation to morality can be rechanneled toward survival in tomorrow.

The logic that informs Ahab's madness but destroys him.

The logic that informs Nemo can well build us homes on far planets circling more safely placed suns. Like Nemo we may well find we need not destroy the horrific whale of reality, we may lurk inside it with machineries, plotting our destinies and going our terror-fraught ways toward an hour when we can lie under those stranger suns and bask easy and breathe light and know peace.

We will probably not choose between these writers, but carry both with us into the future. We will have need of one to question blind Matter and the other to cross-examine blind Man. Thus fused, we shall face the future with fortitude and stamina.

But before we move up in seas of space, the time is now to move sidewise and along and down through seas of water. Here then is Verne's *Twenty Thousand Leagues Under* that *Sea*, his "American" book, his book "moderne," his particular sublime and mad captain, and his strange metal fish.

Portholes tight! Periscope down!

Prepare to submerge.

—RAY BRADBURY

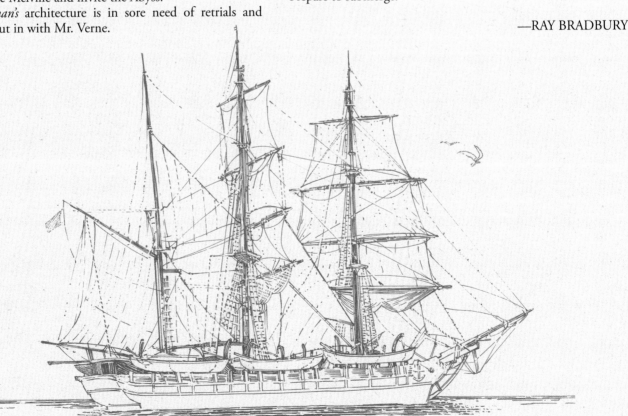

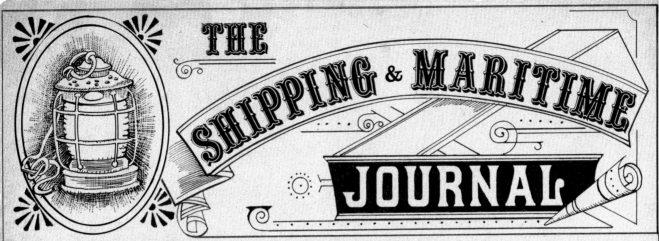

THE SHIPPING & MARITIME JOURNAL

NEW YORK and BOSTON, Sept. 16, 1866

A SHIFTING REEF!

STRANGE SIGHTINGS AT SEA!!

—○—

MERCHANTS, SHIPOWNERS, OTHER SEAFARING PEOPLE DEEPLY CONCERNED!

FACTS ENTERED IN VARIOUS LOGBOOKS AGREE CLOSELY WITH ONE ANOTHER!

The year 1866 was marked by a strange occurrence. Several ships had reported sighting an "enormous thing." The long spindle-shaped object was larger and faster than a whale and occasionally phosphorescent.

On July 20, the steamer Governor Higginson, met a moving mass 5 miles east of Australia. Captain Baker thought at first he was in the presence of an unknown sandbank, when two columns of water shot 150 ft. into the air.

Similar facts were observed on July 23. The Columbus, of the Pacific Steam Navigation Co., sighted a water spouting creature more than 2100 miles away in Pacific waters.

Fifteen days later, 6,000 miles farther off, the Hevetia and the Shannon both sighted the mammal in the Atlantic and estimated its length at more than 350 feet. the latest reports of a collision between the Etna of the Inman Line and the monster have greatly stirred public opinion.

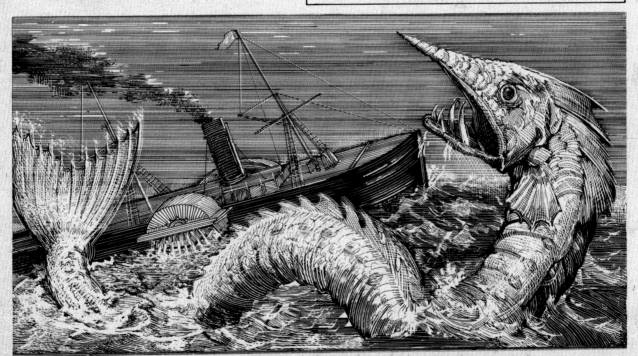

Monster or myth (artist's conception)? The question of the monster has inflamed the minds of the scientific society. Is it an unknown aquatic mammal, the terrible white whale, "Moby Dick," or the legendary Norse Kraken whose tentacles could drag a ship to the bottom of the sea?

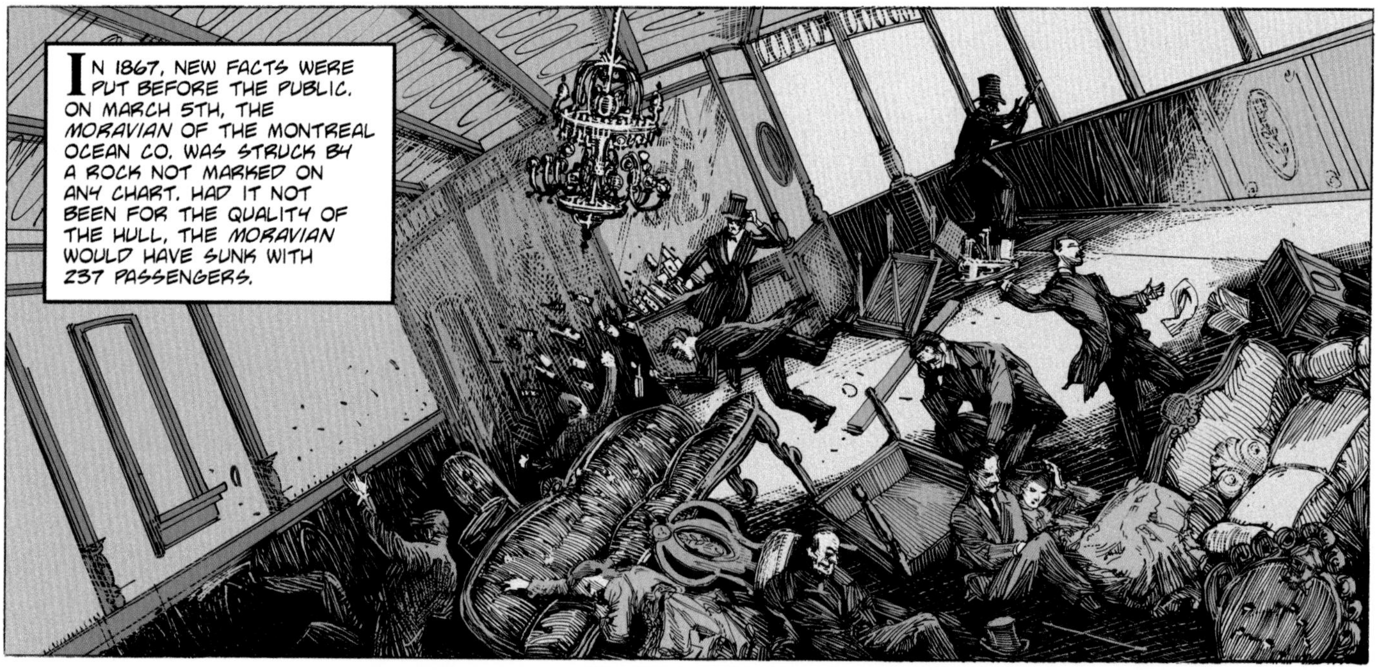
In 1867, new facts were put before the public. On March 5th, the *Moravian* of the Montreal Ocean Co. was struck by a rock not marked on any chart. Had it not been for the quality of the hull, the *Moravian* would have sunk with 237 passengers.

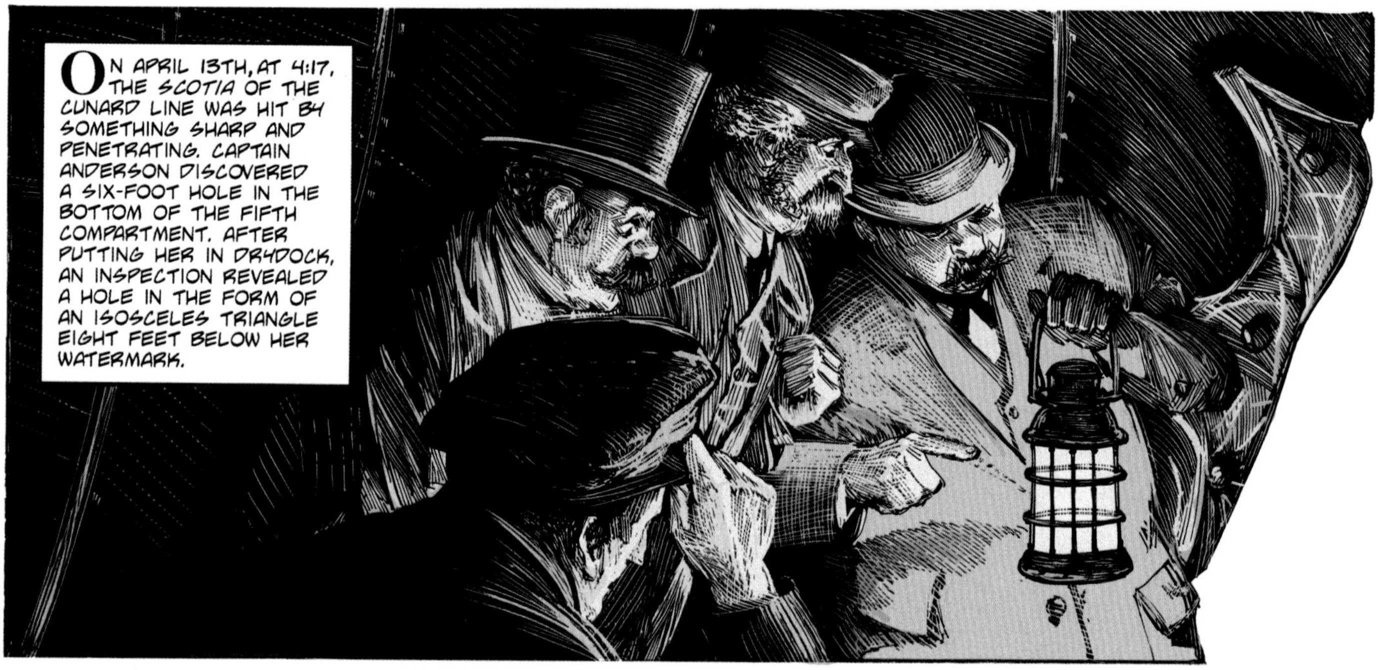
On April 13th, at 4:17, the *Scotia* of the Cunard Line was hit by something sharp and penetrating. Captain Anderson discovered a six-foot hole in the bottom of the fifth compartment. After putting her in drydock, an inspection revealed a hole in the form of an isosceles triangle eight feet below her watermark.

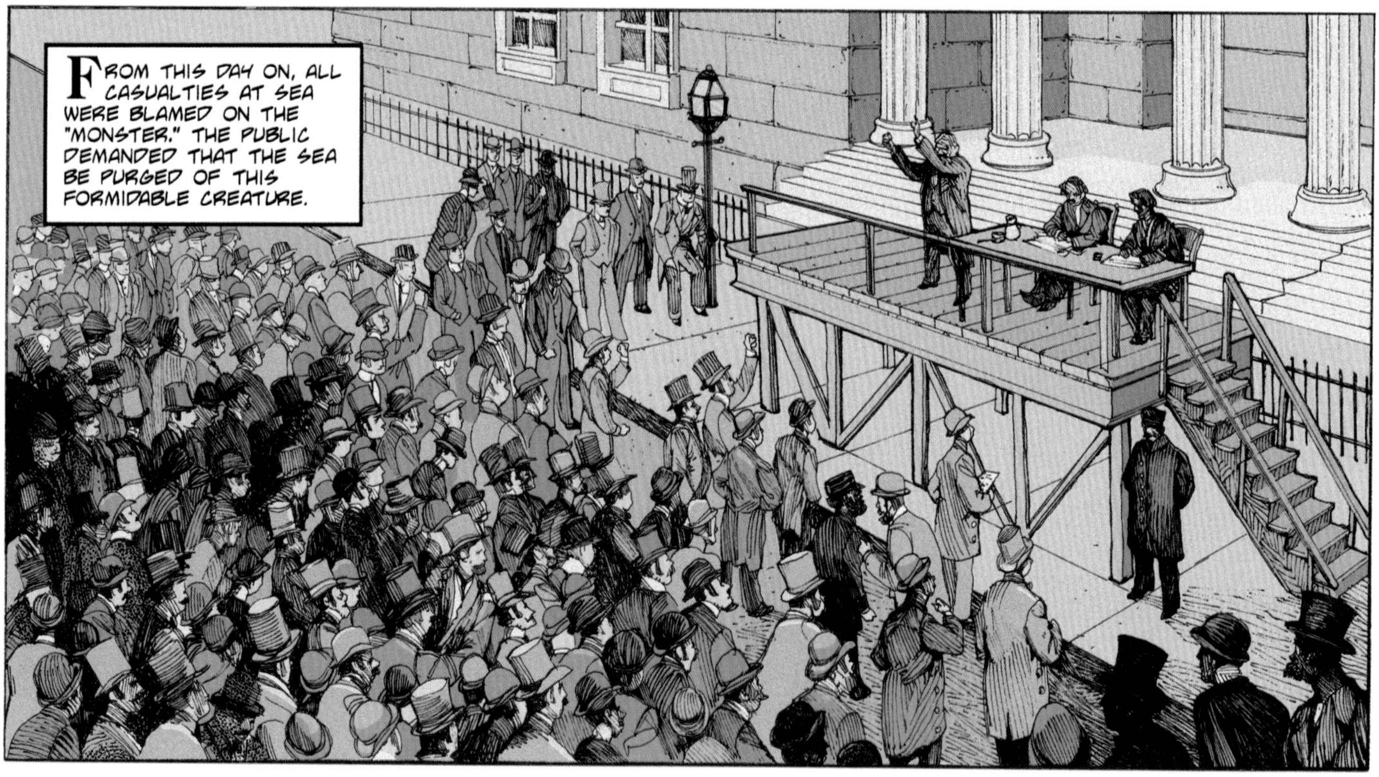
From this day on, all casualties at sea were blamed on the "monster." The public demanded that the sea be purged of this formidable creature.

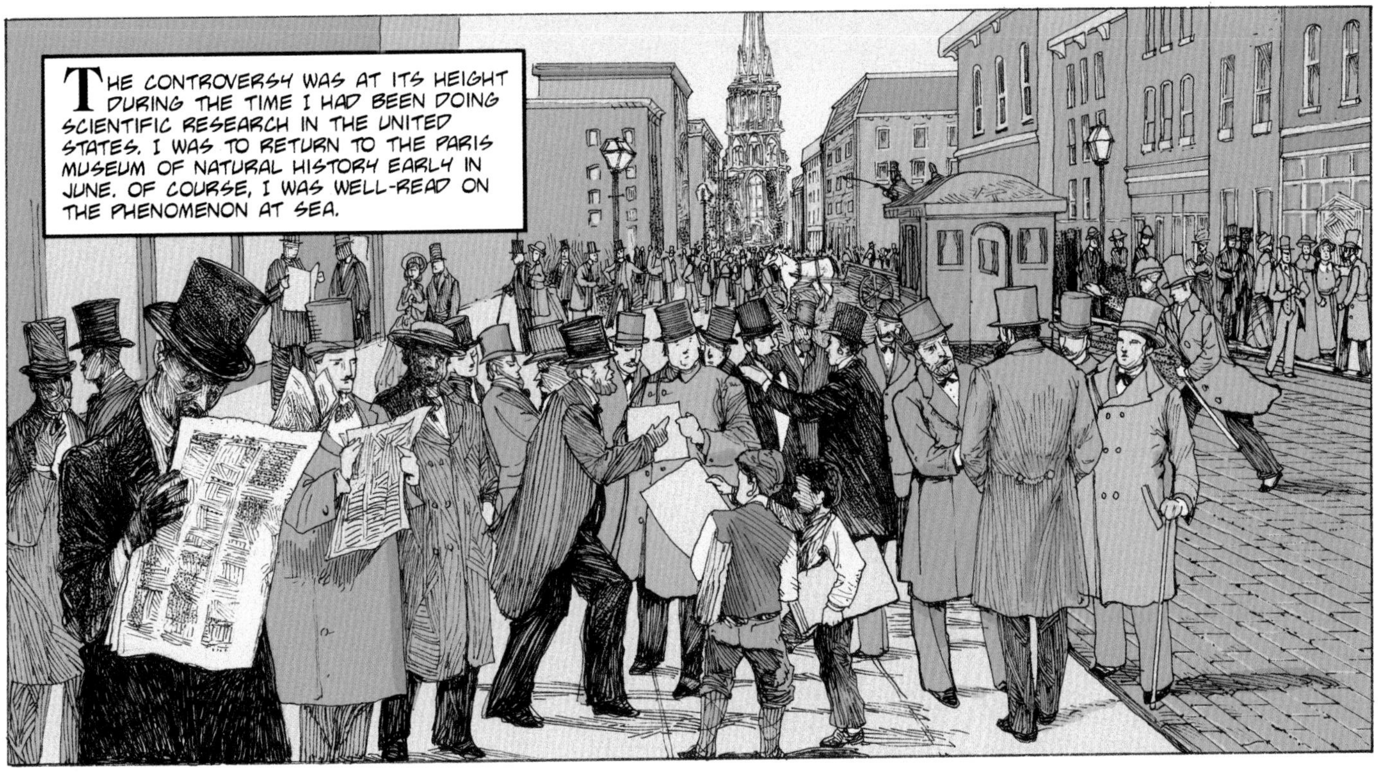
THE CONTROVERSY WAS AT ITS HEIGHT DURING THE TIME I HAD BEEN DOING SCIENTIFIC RESEARCH IN THE UNITED STATES. I WAS TO RETURN TO THE PARIS MUSEUM OF NATURAL HISTORY EARLY IN JUNE. OF COURSE, I WAS WELL-READ ON THE PHENOMENON AT SEA.

IN FRANCE, I HAD PUBLISHED A TWO-VOLUME WORK, "MYSTERIES OF THE OCEAN DEPTHS," WHICH HAD GAINED FOR ME AN INTERNATIONAL REPUTATION.

SEVERAL NEW YORK PAPERS ASKED FOR MY OPINION. THERE WERE TWO POSSIBLE SOLUTIONS: A MARINE ANIMAL OF COLOSSAL STRENGTH...

...OR SOME SORT OF SUBMARINE. A COUNTRY MIGHT TRY TO BUILD SUCH A DEVICE, BUT HOW COULD ITS CONSTRUCTION FAIL TO ESCAPE PUBLIC NOTICE?

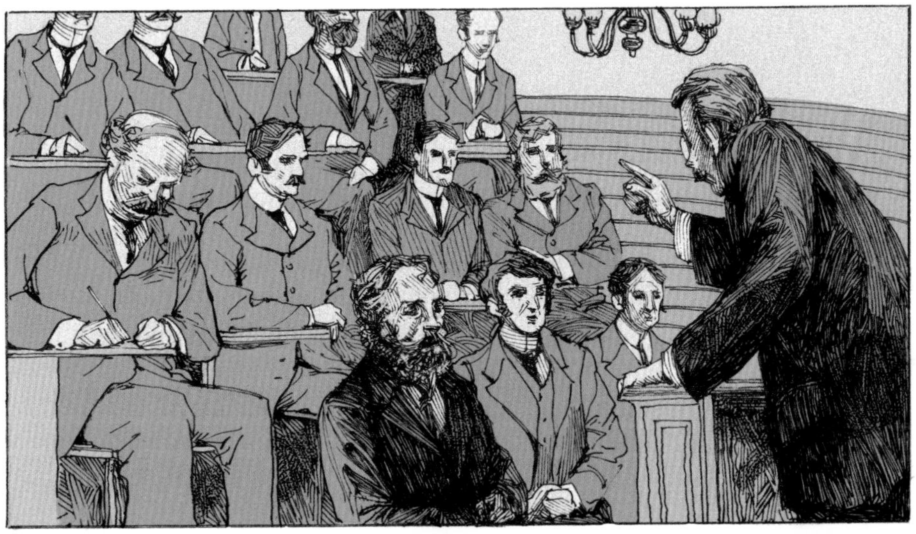

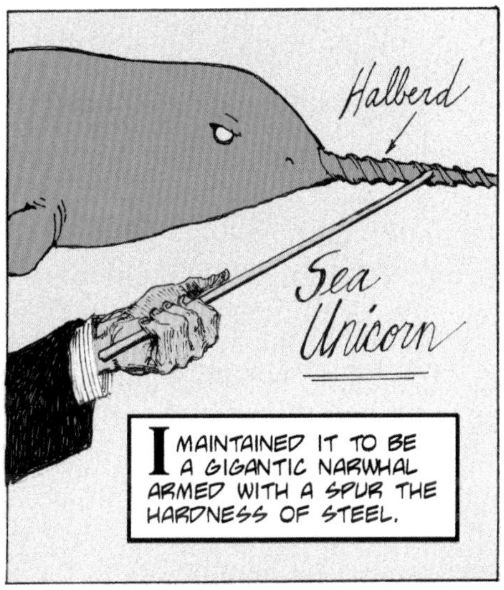
Halberd
Sea Unicorn
I MAINTAINED IT TO BE A GIGANTIC NARWHAL ARMED WITH A SPUR THE HARDNESS OF STEEL.

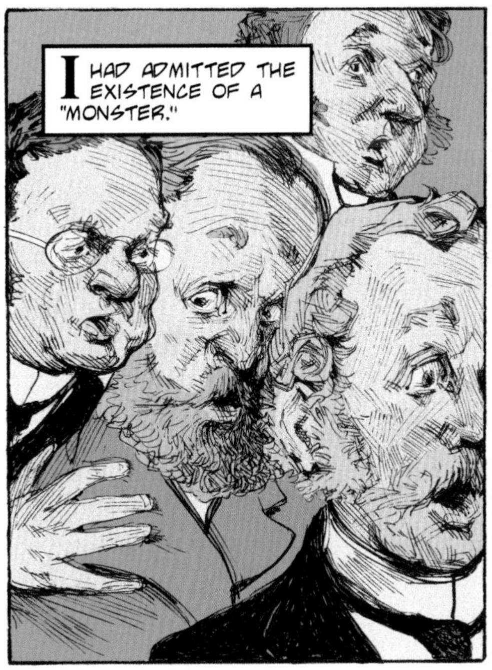
I HAD ADMITTED THE EXISTENCE OF A "MONSTER."

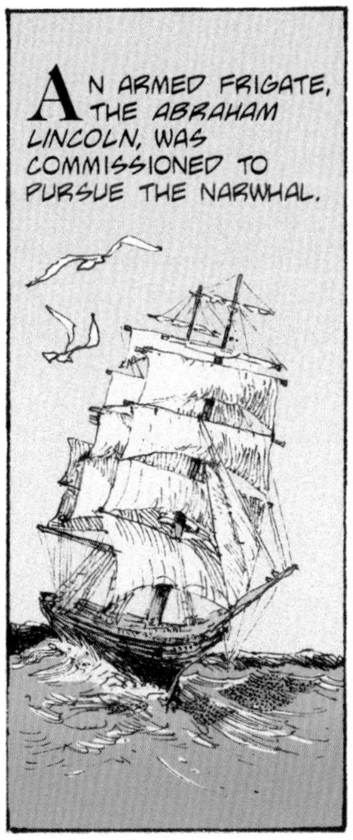
AN ARMED FRIGATE, THE *ABRAHAM LINCOLN*, WAS COMMISSIONED TO PURSUE THE NARWHAL.

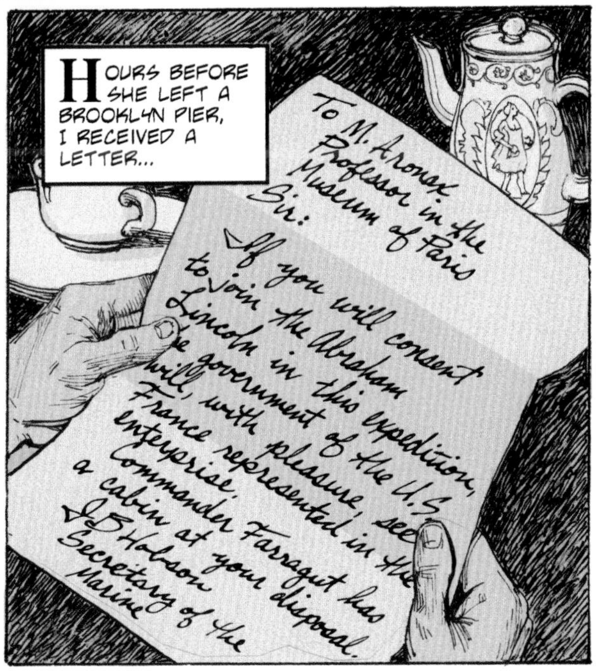
HOURS BEFORE SHE LEFT A BROOKLYN PIER, I RECEIVED A LETTER...
To M. Aronax
Professor in the
Museum of Paris
Sir:
If you will consent
to join the Abraham
Lincoln in this expedition,
the government of the U.S.
will, with pleasure, see
France represented in the
enterprise.
Commander Farragut has
a cabin at your disposal.
J.B. Hobson
Secretary of the
Marine

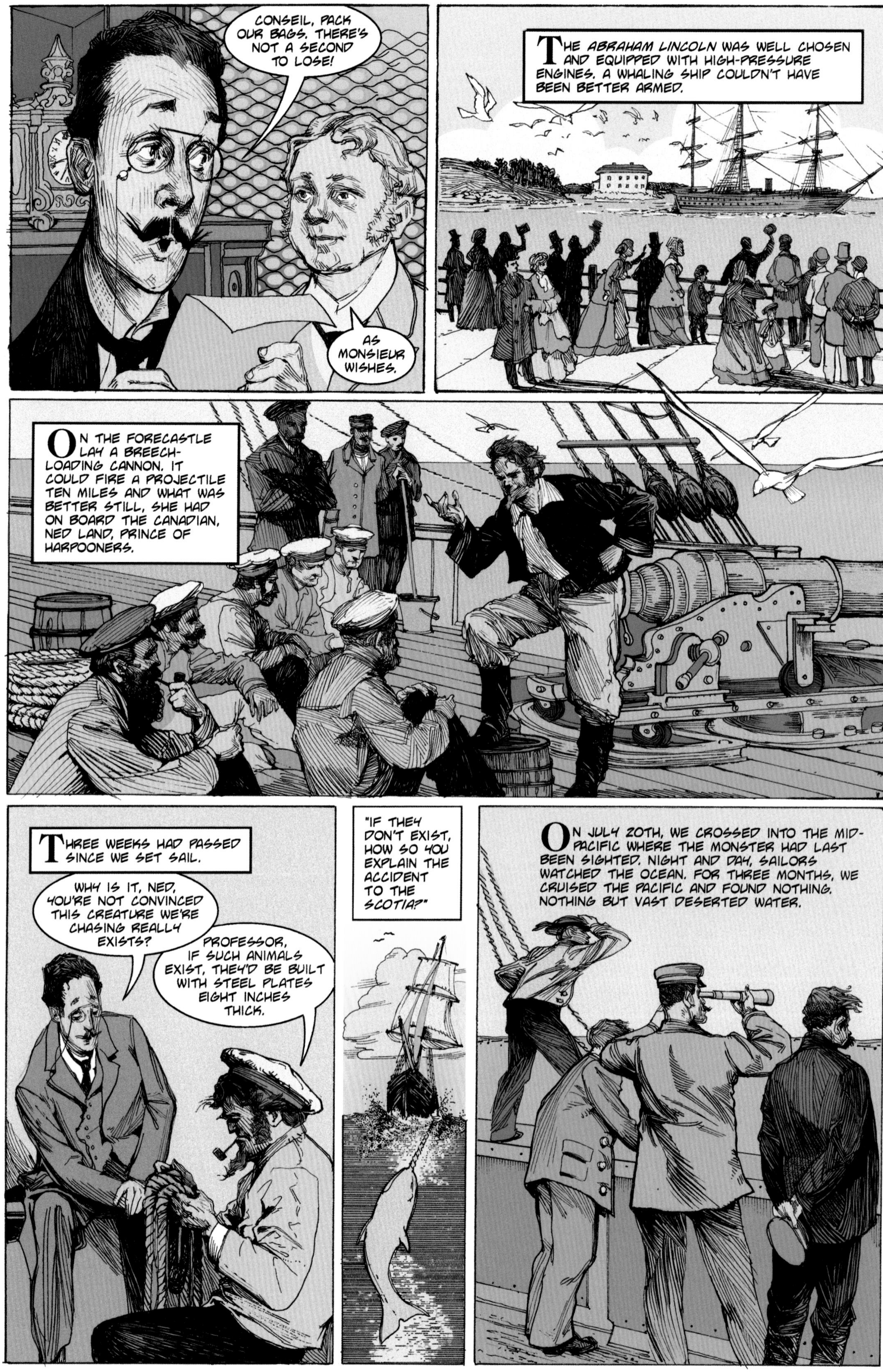
CONSEIL, PACK OUR BAGS. THERE'S NOT A SECOND TO LOSE!
AS MONSIEUR WISHES.
THE *ABRAHAM LINCOLN* WAS WELL CHOSEN AND EQUIPPED WITH HIGH-PRESSURE ENGINES. A WHALING SHIP COULDN'T HAVE BEEN BETTER ARMED.
ON THE FORECASTLE LAY A BREECH-LOADING CANNON. IT COULD FIRE A PROJECTILE TEN MILES AND WHAT WAS BETTER STILL, SHE HAD ON BOARD THE CANADIAN, NED LAND, PRINCE OF HARPOONERS.
THREE WEEKS HAD PASSED SINCE WE SET SAIL.
WHY IS IT, NED, YOU'RE NOT CONVINCED THIS CREATURE WE'RE CHASING REALLY EXISTS?
PROFESSOR, IF SUCH ANIMALS EXIST, THEY'D BE BUILT WITH STEEL PLATES EIGHT INCHES THICK.
"IF THEY DON'T EXIST, HOW SO YOU EXPLAIN THE ACCIDENT TO THE *SCOTIA*?"
ON JULY 20TH, WE CROSSED INTO THE MID-PACIFIC WHERE THE MONSTER HAD LAST BEEN SIGHTED. NIGHT AND DAY, SAILORS WATCHED THE OCEAN. FOR THREE MONTHS, WE CRUISED THE PACIFIC AND FOUND NOTHING. NOTHING BUT VAST DESERTED WATER.

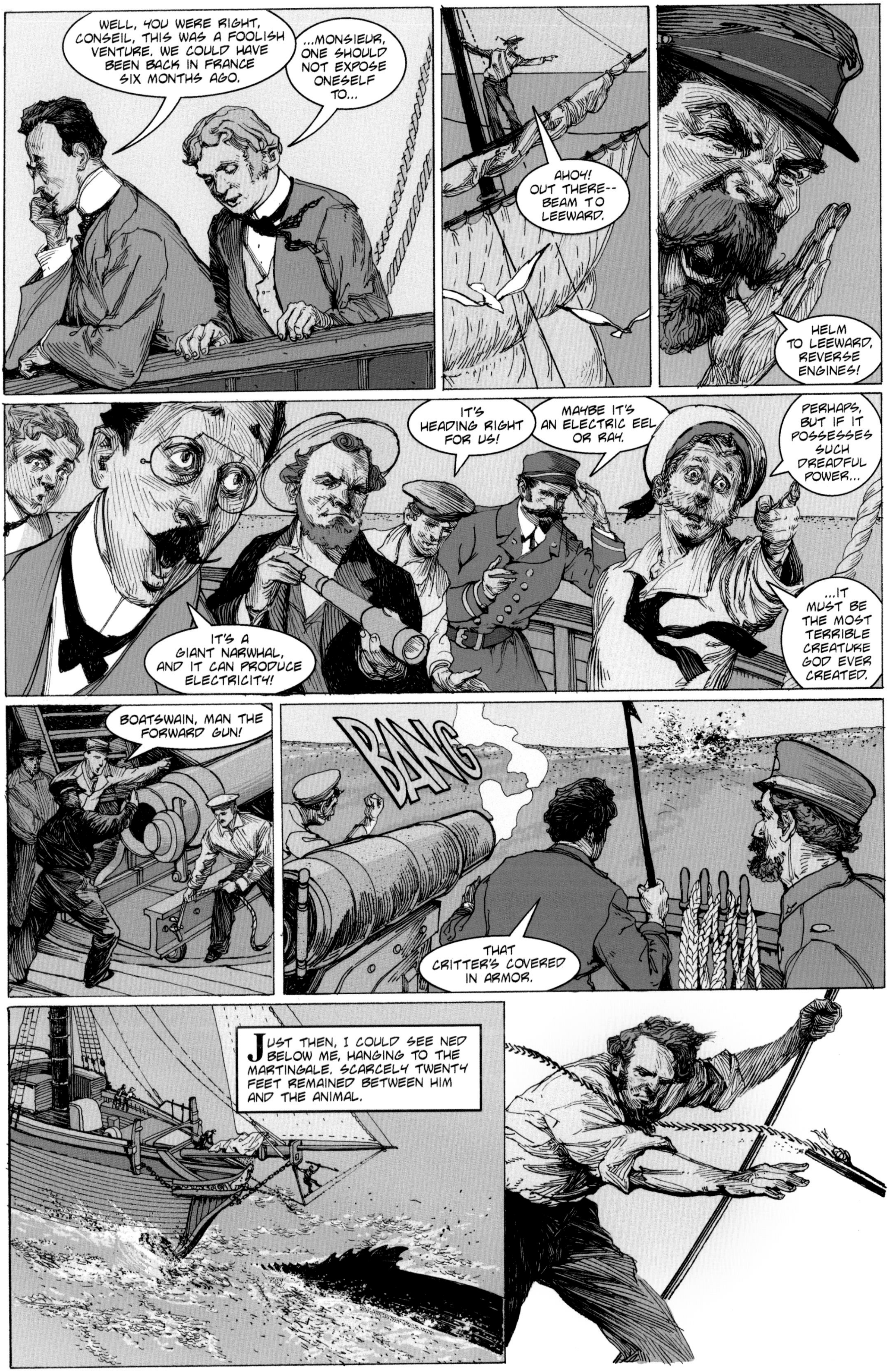
WELL, YOU WERE RIGHT, CONSEIL, THIS WAS A FOOLISH VENTURE. WE COULD HAVE BEEN BACK IN FRANCE SIX MONTHS AGO.
...MONSIEUR, ONE SHOULD NOT EXPOSE ONESELF TO...
AHOY! OUT THERE-- BEAM TO LEEWARD.
HELM TO LEEWARD, REVERSE ENGINES!
IT'S A GIANT NARWHAL, AND IT CAN PRODUCE ELECTRICITY!
IT'S HEADING RIGHT FOR US!
MAYBE IT'S AN ELECTRIC EEL OR RAY.
PERHAPS, BUT IF IT POSSESSES SUCH DREADFUL POWER...
...IT MUST BE THE MOST TERRIBLE CREATURE GOD EVER CREATED.
BOATSWAIN, MAN THE FORWARD GUN!
BANG
THAT CRITTER'S COVERED IN ARMOR.
JUST THEN, I COULD SEE NED BELOW ME, HANGING TO THE MARTINGALE. SCARCELY TWENTY FEET REMAINED BETWEEN HIM AND THE ANIMAL.

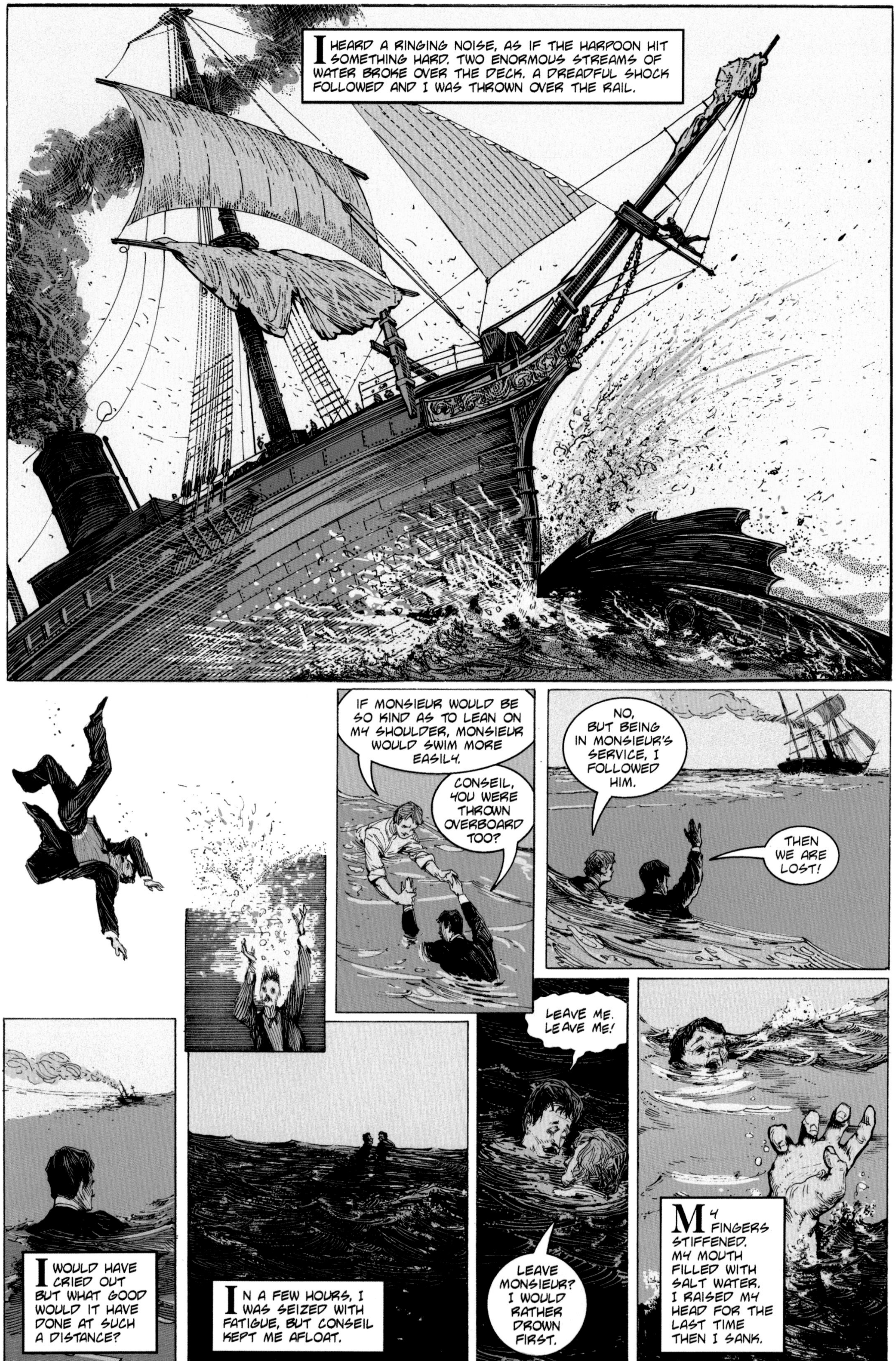
I heard a ringing noise, as if the harpoon hit something hard. Two enormous streams of water broke over the deck. A dreadful shock followed and I was thrown over the rail.
If monsieur would be so kind as to lean on my shoulder, monsieur would swim more easily.
Conseil, you were thrown overboard too?
No, but being in monsieur's service, I followed him.
Then we are lost!
I would have cried out but what good would it have done at such a distance?
In a few hours, I was seized with fatigue, but Conseil kept me afloat.
Leave me. Leave me!
Leave monsieur? I would rather drown first.
My fingers stiffened. My mouth filled with salt water. I raised my head for the last time then I sank.

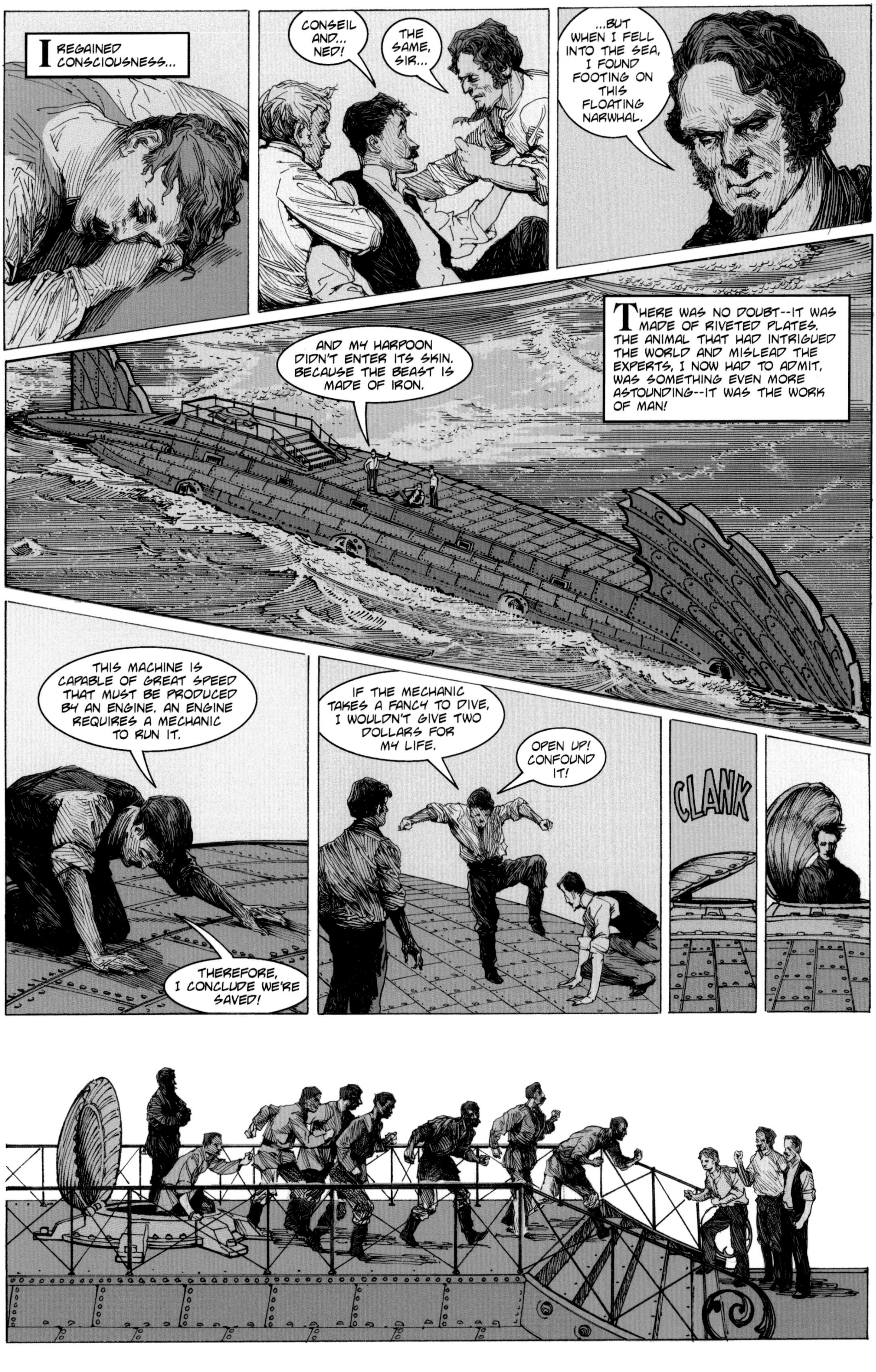
I REGAINED CONSCIOUSNESS...
CONSEIL AND... NED!
THE SAME, SIR...
...BUT WHEN I FELL INTO THE SEA, I FOUND FOOTING ON THIS FLOATING NARWHAL.
THERE WAS NO DOUBT--IT WAS MADE OF RIVETED PLATES. THE ANIMAL THAT HAD INTRIGUED THE WORLD AND MISLEAD THE EXPERTS, I NOW HAD TO ADMIT, WAS SOMETHING EVEN MORE ASTOUNDING--IT WAS THE WORK OF MAN!
AND MY HARPOON DIDN'T ENTER ITS SKIN. BECAUSE THE BEAST IS MADE OF IRON.
THIS MACHINE IS CAPABLE OF GREAT SPEED THAT MUST BE PRODUCED BY AN ENGINE. AN ENGINE REQUIRES A MECHANIC TO RUN IT.
THEREFORE, I CONCLUDE WE'RE SAVED!
IF THE MECHANIC TAKES A FANCY TO DIVE, I WOULDN'T GIVE TWO DOLLARS FOR MY LIFE.
OPEN UP! CONFOUND IT!
CLANK

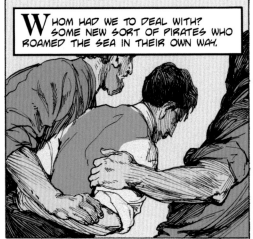

WHOM HAD WE TO DEAL WITH? SOME NEW SORT OF PIRATES WHO ROAMED THE SEA IN THEIR OWN WAY.

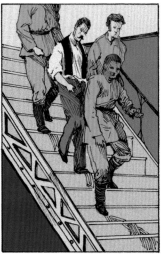

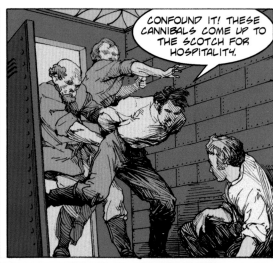

CONFOUND IT! THESE CANNIBALS COME UP TO THE SCOTCH FOR HOSPITALITY.

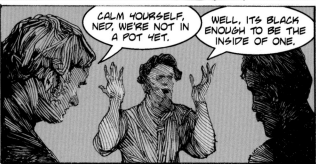

CALM YOURSELF, NED, WE'RE NOT IN A POT YET.

WELL, IT'S BLACK ENOUGH TO BE THE INSIDE OF ONE.

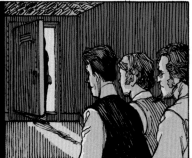

NED WAS RIGHT. THE THREE OF US WERE LOCKED IN AN IRON ROOM. HALF AN HOUR PASSED WITHOUT OUR SITUATION CHANGING, WHEN SUDDENLY THE LIGHT WENT ON...

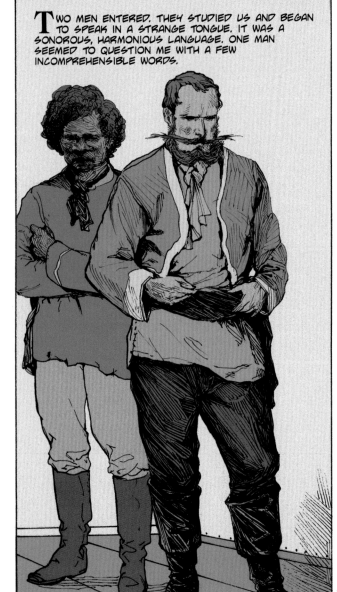

TWO MEN ENTERED. THEY STUDIED US AND BEGAN TO SPEAK IN A STRANGE TONGUE. IT WAS A SONOROUS, HARMONIOUS LANGUAGE. ONE MAN SEEMED TO QUESTION ME WITH A FEW INCOMPREHENSIBLE WORDS.

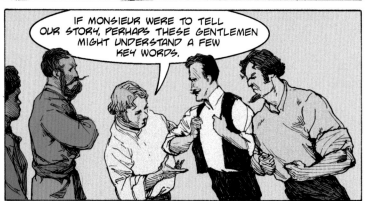

IF MONSIEUR WERE TO TELL OUR STORY, PERHAPS THESE GENTLEMEN MIGHT UNDERSTAND A FEW KEY WORDS.

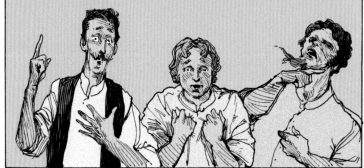

I RECITED OUR ADVENTURE, PRONOUNCING EACH WORD CAREFULLY. THE TALL MAN LISTENED WHILE I REPEATED THE STORY IN LATIN, BUT NOTHING IN HIS EXPRESSION SHOWED THAT HE UNDERSTOOD A WORD. CONSEIL TRIED AGAIN, SPEAKING GERMAN AND NED FOLLOWED IN ENGLISH, BUT TO NO AVAIL.

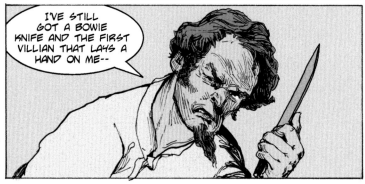

I'VE STILL GOT A BOWIE KNIFE AND THE FIRST VILLIAN THAT LAYS A HAND ON ME--

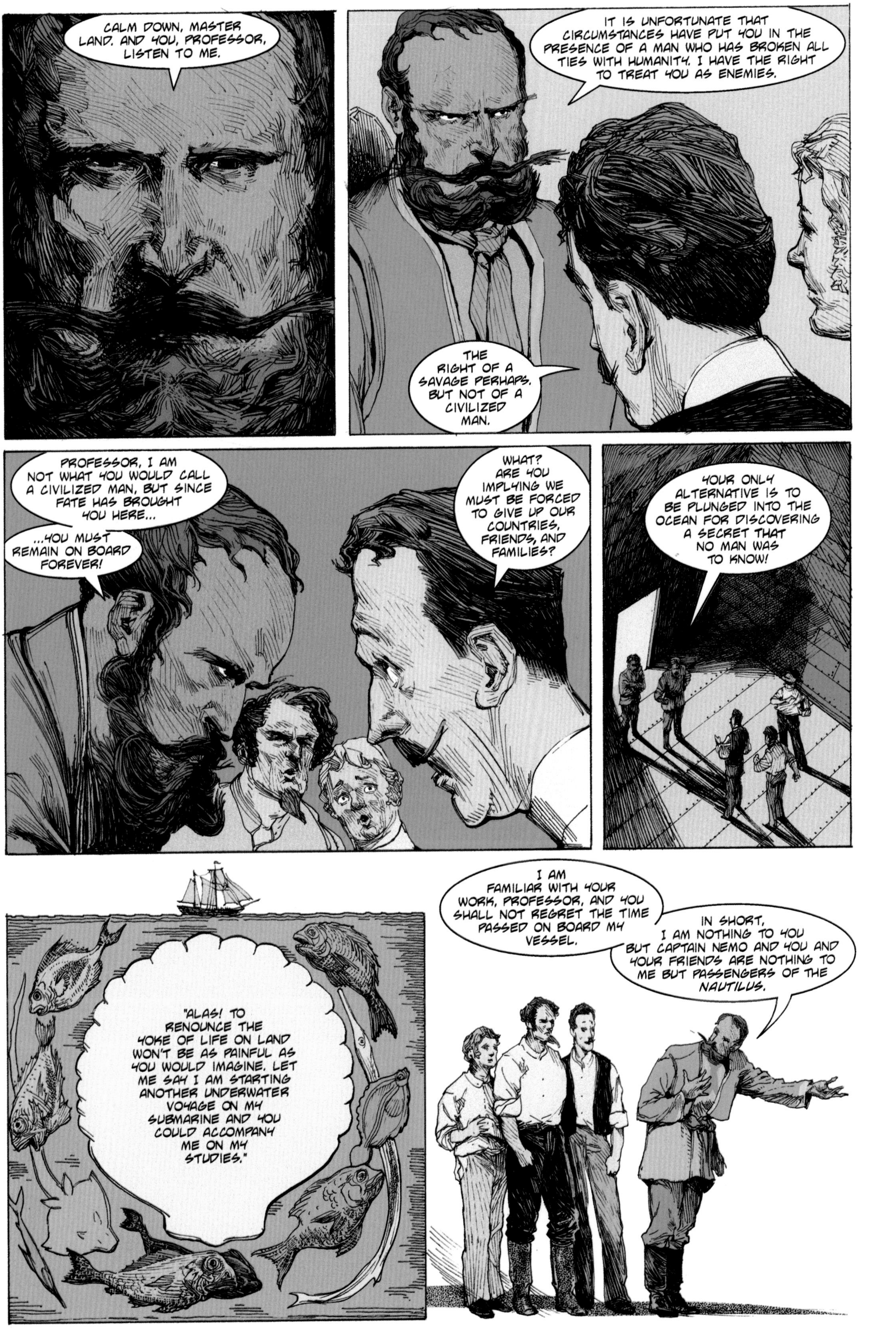

CALM DOWN, MASTER LAND. AND YOU, PROFESSOR, LISTEN TO ME.
IT IS UNFORTUNATE THAT CIRCUMSTANCES HAVE PUT YOU IN THE PRESENCE OF A MAN WHO HAS BROKEN ALL TIES WITH HUMANITY. I HAVE THE RIGHT TO TREAT YOU AS ENEMIES.
THE RIGHT OF A SAVAGE PERHAPS. BUT NOT OF A CIVILIZED MAN.
PROFESSOR, I AM NOT WHAT YOU WOULD CALL A CIVILIZED MAN, BUT SINCE FATE HAS BROUGHT YOU HERE...
...YOU MUST REMAIN ON BOARD FOREVER!
WHAT? ARE YOU IMPLYING WE MUST BE FORCED TO GIVE UP OUR COUNTRIES, FRIENDS, AND FAMILIES?
YOUR ONLY ALTERNATIVE IS TO BE PLUNGED INTO THE OCEAN FOR DISCOVERING A SECRET THAT NO MAN WAS TO KNOW!
"ALAS! TO RENOUNCE THE YOKE OF LIFE ON LAND WON'T BE AS PAINFUL AS YOU WOULD IMAGINE. LET ME SAY I AM STARTING ANOTHER UNDERWATER VOYAGE ON MY SUBMARINE AND YOU COULD ACCOMPANY ME ON MY STUDIES."
I AM FAMILIAR WITH YOUR WORK, PROFESSOR, AND YOU SHALL NOT REGRET THE TIME PASSED ON BOARD MY VESSEL.
IN SHORT, I AM NOTHING TO YOU BUT CAPTAIN NEMO AND YOU AND YOUR FRIENDS ARE NOTHING TO ME BUT PASSENGERS OF THE *NAUTILUS*.

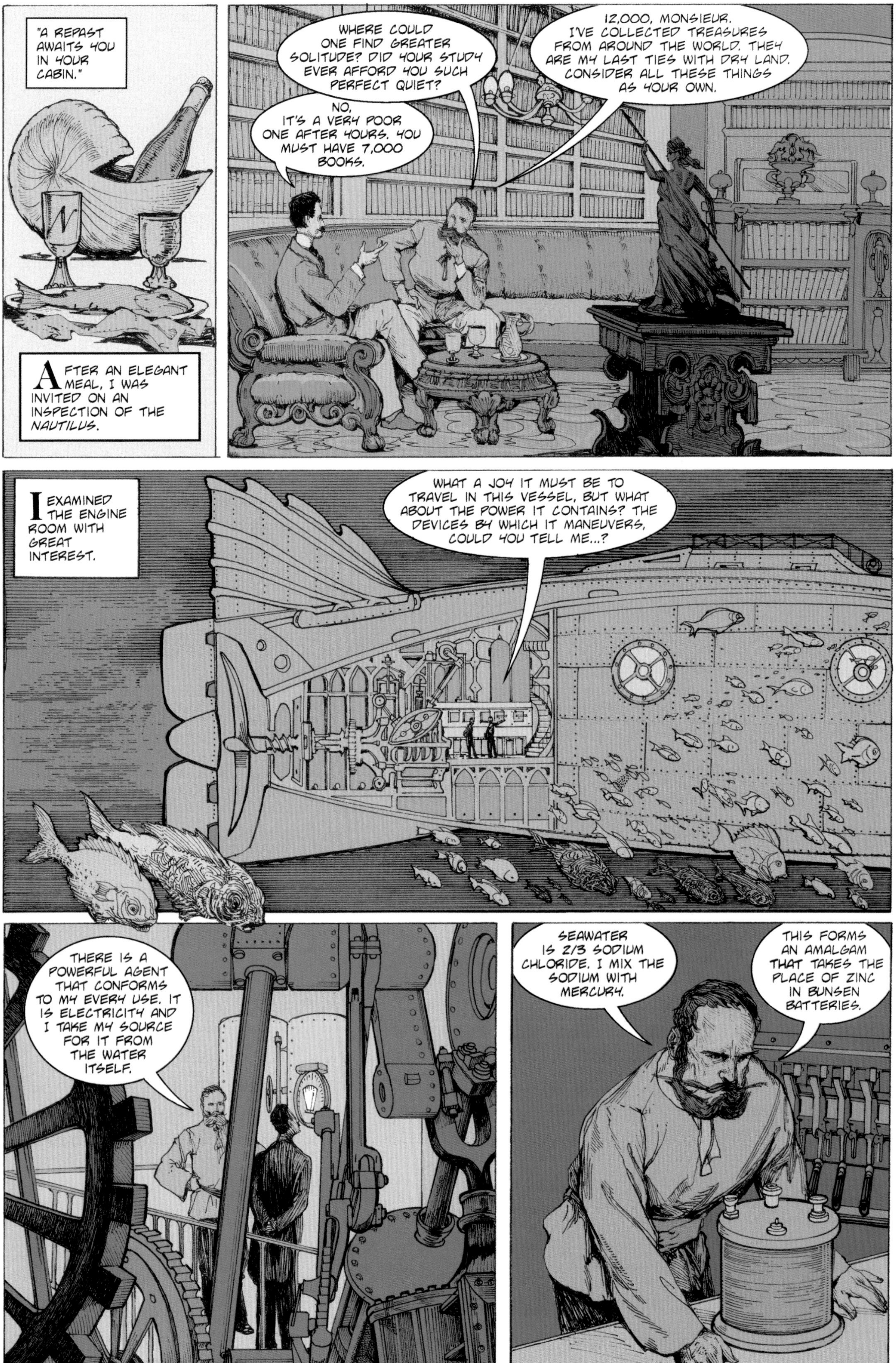
"A REPAST AWAITS YOU IN YOUR CABIN."
AFTER AN ELEGANT MEAL, I WAS INVITED ON AN INSPECTION OF THE *NAUTILUS*.
WHERE COULD ONE FIND GREATER SOLITUDE? DID YOUR STUDY EVER AFFORD YOU SUCH PERFECT QUIET?
NO, IT'S A VERY POOR ONE AFTER HOURS. YOU MUST HAVE 7,000 BOOKS.
12,000, MONSIEUR. I'VE COLLECTED TREASURES FROM AROUND THE WORLD. THEY ARE MY LAST TIES WITH DRY LAND. CONSIDER ALL THESE THINGS AS YOUR OWN.
I EXAMINED THE ENGINE ROOM WITH GREAT INTEREST.
WHAT A JOY IT MUST BE TO TRAVEL IN THIS VESSEL, BUT WHAT ABOUT THE POWER IT CONTAINS? THE DEVICES BY WHICH IT MANEUVERS, COULD YOU TELL ME...?
THERE IS A POWERFUL AGENT THAT CONFORMS TO MY EVERY USE. IT IS ELECTRICITY AND I TAKE MY SOURCE FOR IT FROM THE WATER ITSELF.
SEAWATER IS 2/3 SODIUM CHLORIDE. I MIX THE SODIUM WITH MERCURY.
THIS FORMS AN AMALGAM THAT TAKES THE PLACE OF ZINC IN BUNSEN BATTERIES.

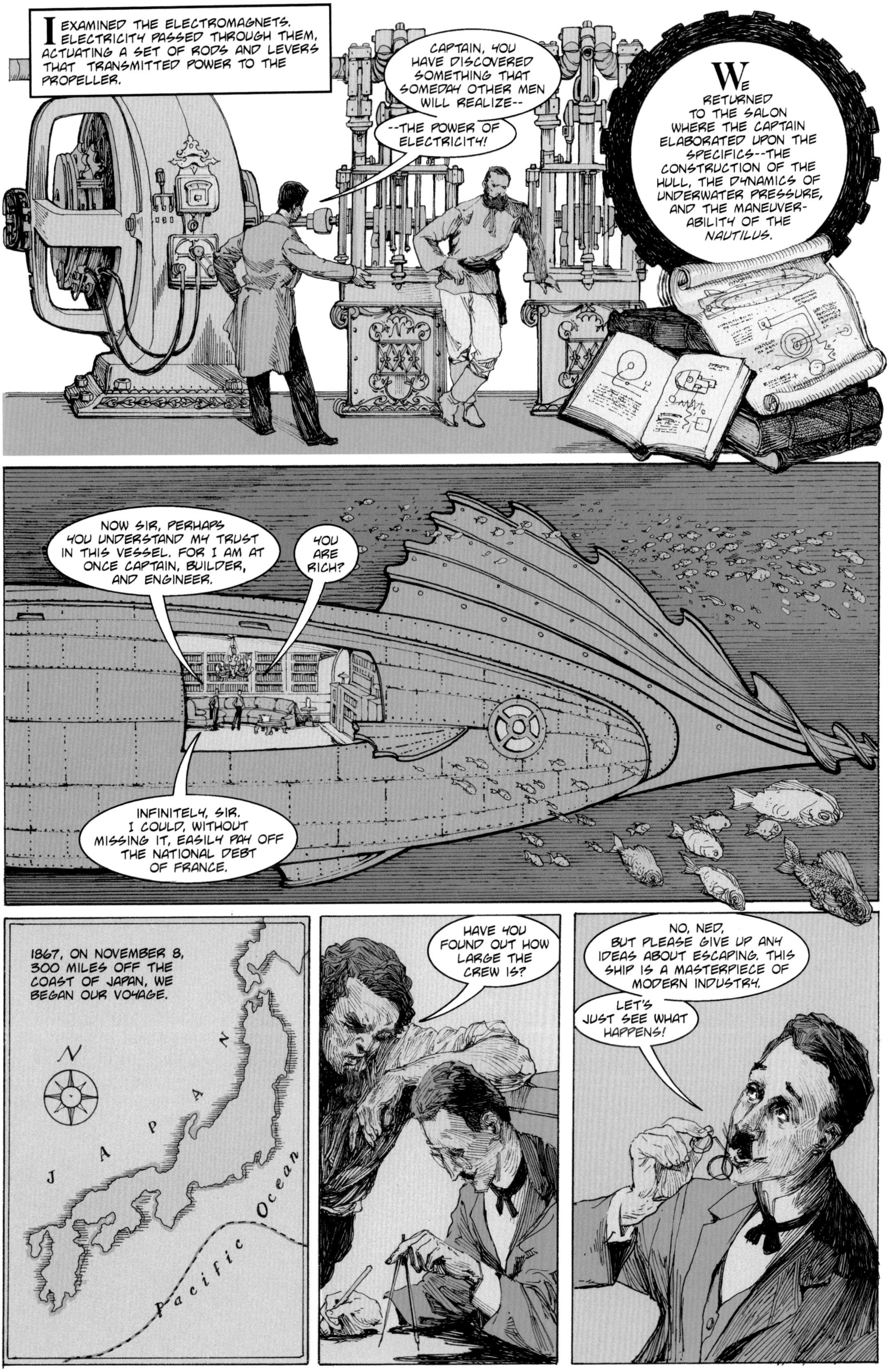
I EXAMINED THE ELECTROMAGNETS. ELECTRICITY PASSED THROUGH THEM, ACTUATING A SET OF RODS AND LEVERS THAT TRANSMITTED POWER TO THE PROPELLER.
CAPTAIN, YOU HAVE DISCOVERED SOMETHING THAT SOMEDAY OTHER MEN WILL REALIZE--
--THE POWER OF ELECTRICITY!
WE RETURNED TO THE SALON WHERE THE CAPTAIN ELABORATED UPON THE SPECIFICS--THE CONSTRUCTION OF THE HULL, THE DYNAMICS OF UNDERWATER PRESSURE, AND THE MANEUVER-ABILITY OF THE *NAUTILUS*.
NOW SIR, PERHAPS YOU UNDERSTAND MY TRUST IN THIS VESSEL. FOR I AM AT ONCE CAPTAIN, BUILDER, AND ENGINEER.
YOU ARE RICH?
INFINITELY, SIR. I COULD, WITHOUT MISSING IT, EASILY PAY OFF THE NATIONAL DEBT OF FRANCE.
1867, ON NOVEMBER 8, 300 MILES OFF THE COAST OF JAPAN, WE BEGAN OUR VOYAGE.
N
JAPAN
Pacific Ocean
HAVE YOU FOUND OUT HOW LARGE THE CREW IS?
NO, NED, BUT PLEASE GIVE UP ANY IDEAS ABOUT ESCAPING. THIS SHIP IS A MASTERPIECE OF MODERN INDUSTRY.
LET'S JUST SEE WHAT HAPPENS!

ON NOVEMBER 16, THE CAPTAIN INVITED US ON A HUNTING PARTY IN THE UNDERWATER FORESTS OF CRESPO ISLAND. HE HAD PERFECTED AN UNDERWATER BREATHING APPARATUS AND A REMARKABLE AIR GUN THAT SHOT ELECTRICAL BULLETS.

CONSEIL AND I STOPPED MANY TIMES THROUGHOUT THE EXCURSION TO CLASSIFY SPECIMENS OF ZOOPHYTES AND MOLLUSKS. HOW I WOULD HAVE ENJOYED, LIKE CAPTAIN NEMO AND HIS COMPANION, TO HAVE EXCHANGED THOUGHTS BY MEANS OF PREVIOUSLY ARRANGED HAND SIGNALS. I TALKED TO MYSELF, SHOUTING INSIDE MY HELMET AND PERHAPS WASTING MORE AIR THAN I SHOULD HAVE WITH MY VAIN WORDS.

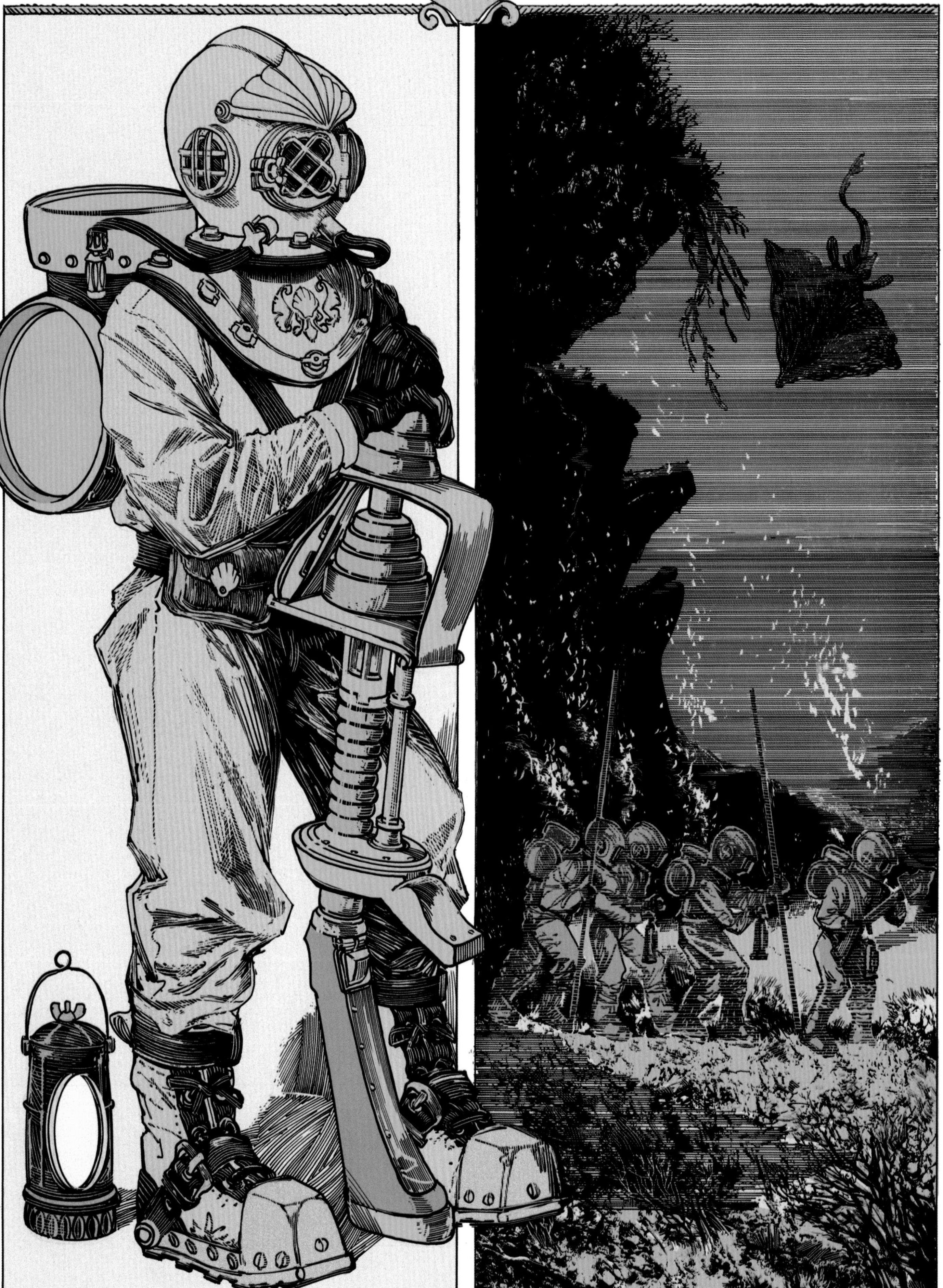

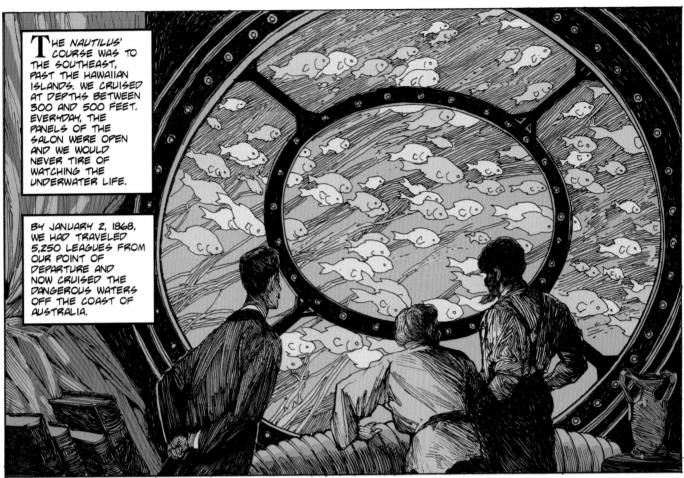

THE *NAUTILUS'* COURSE WAS TO THE SOUTHEAST, PAST THE HAWAIIAN ISLANDS. WE CRUISED AT DEPTHS BETWEEN 300 AND 500 FEET. EVERYDAY, THE PANELS OF THE SALON WERE OPEN AND WE WOULD NEVER TIRE OF WATCHING THE UNDERWATER LIFE.

BY JANUARY 2, 1868, WE HAD TRAVELED 5,250 LEAGUES FROM OUR POINT OF DEPARTURE AND NOW CRUISED THE DANGEROUS WATERS OFF THE COAST OF AUSTRALIA.

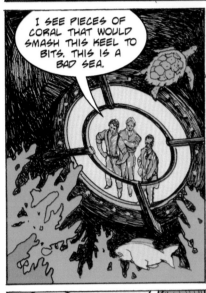

I SEE PIECES OF CORAL THAT WOULD SMASH THIS KEEL TO BITS. THIS IS A BAD SEA.

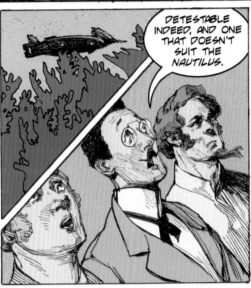

DETESTABLE INDEED, AND ONE THAT DOESN'T SUIT THE *NAUTILUS.*

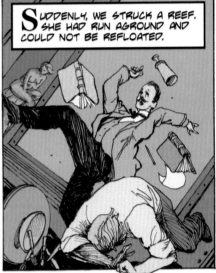

SUDDENLY, WE STRUCK A REEF. SHE HAD RUN AGROUND AND COULD NOT BE REFLOATED.

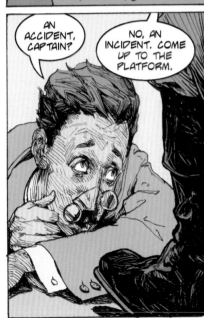

AN ACCIDENT, CAPTAIN?

NO, AN INCIDENT. COME UP TO THE PLATFORM.

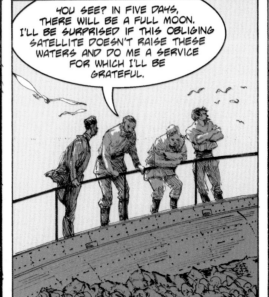

YOU SEE? IN FIVE DAYS, THERE WILL BE A FULL MOON. I'LL BE SURPRISED IF THIS OBLIGING SATELLITE DOESN'T RAISE THESE WATERS AND DO ME A SERVICE FOR WHICH I'LL BE GRATEFUL.

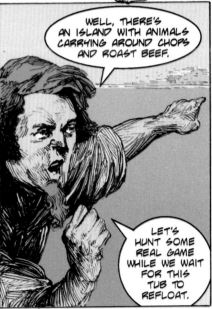

WELL, THERE'S AN ISLAND WITH ANIMALS CARRYING AROUND CHOPS AND ROAST BEEF.

LET'S HUNT SOME REAL GAME WHILE WE WAIT FOR THIS TUB TO REFLOAT.

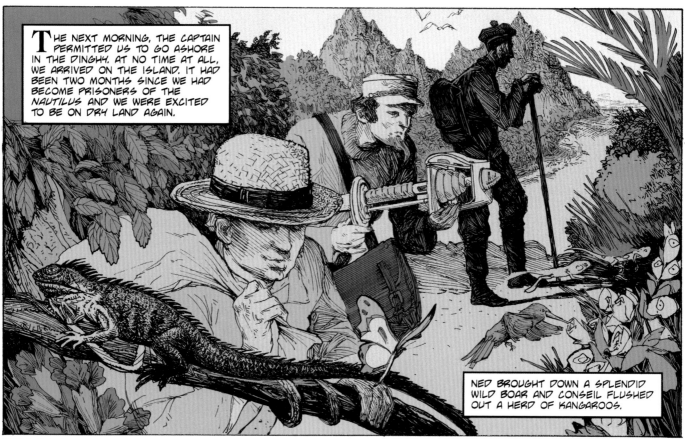

THE NEXT MORNING, THE CAPTAIN PERMITTED US TO GO ASHORE IN THE DINGHY. AT NO TIME AT ALL, WE ARRIVED ON THE ISLAND. IT HAD BEEN TWO MONTHS SINCE WE HAD BECOME PRISONERS OF THE *NAUTILUS* AND WE WERE EXCITED TO BE ON DRY LAND AGAIN.

NED BROUGHT DOWN A SPLENDID WILD BOAR AND CONSEIL FLUSHED OUT A HERD OF KANGAROOS.

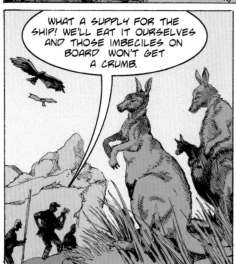

WHAT A SUPPLY FOR THE SHIP! WE'LL EAT IT OURSELVES AND THOSE IMBECILES ON BOARD WON'T GET A CRUMB.

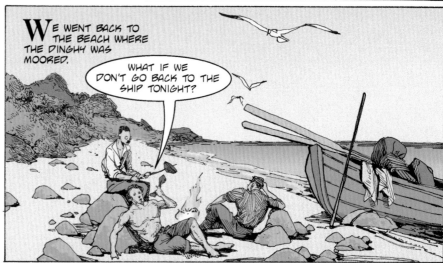

WE WENT BACK TO THE BEACH WHERE THE DINGHY WAS MOORED.

WHAT IF WE DON'T GO BACK TO THE SHIP TONIGHT?

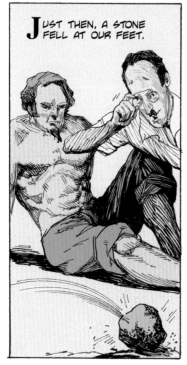

JUST THEN, A STONE FELL AT OUR FEET.

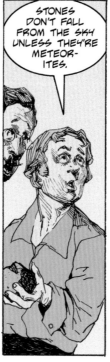

STONES DON'T FALL FROM THE SKY UNLESS THEY'RE METEOR-ITES.

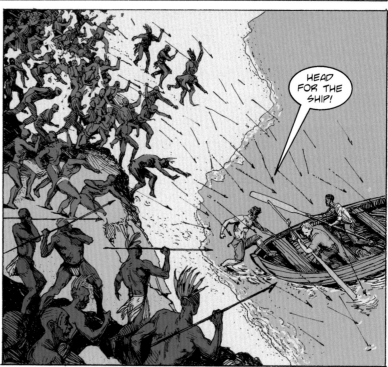

HEAD FOR THE SHIP!

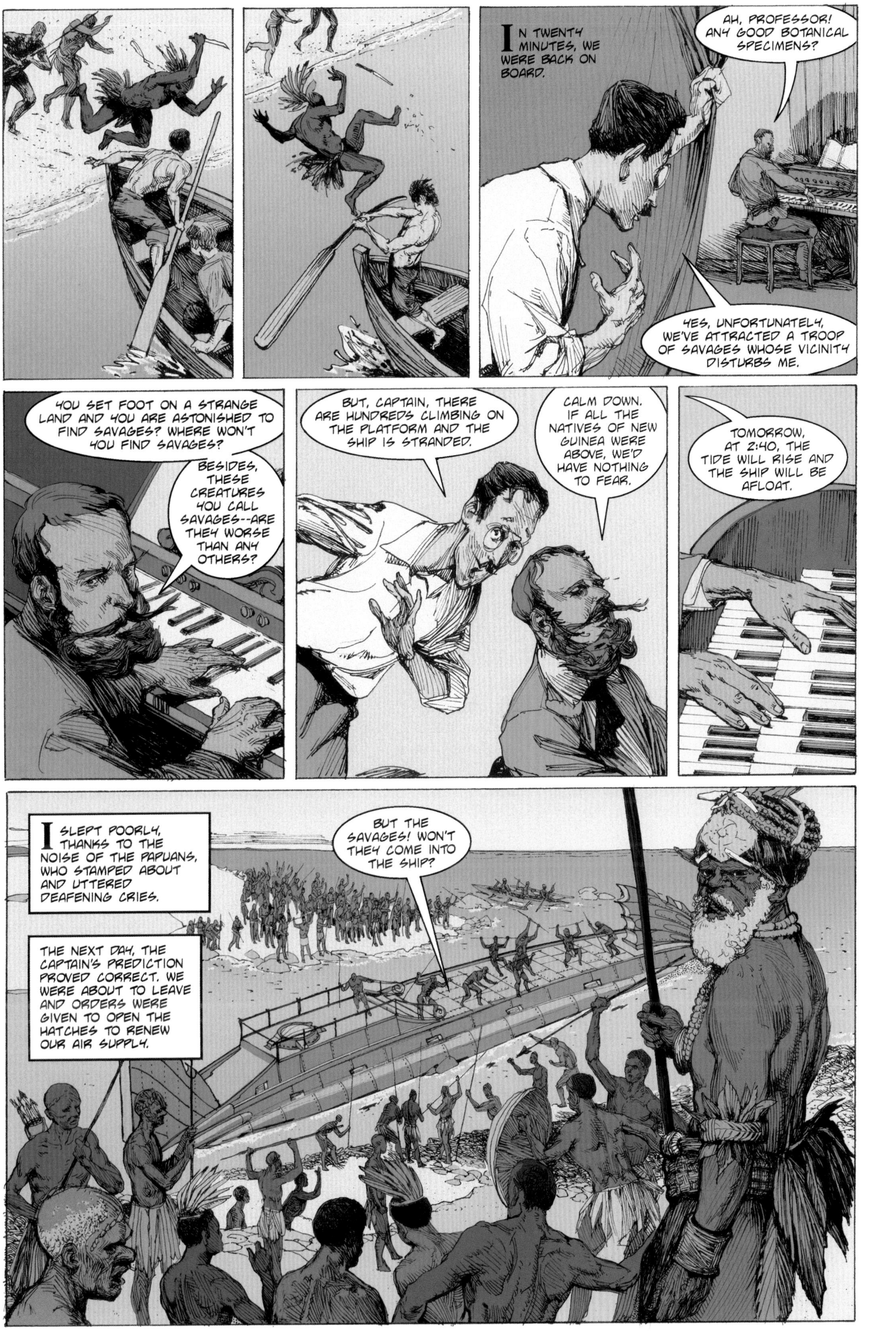
IN TWENTY MINUTES, WE WERE BACK ON BOARD.
AH, PROFESSOR! ANY GOOD BOTANICAL SPECIMENS?
YES, UNFORTUNATELY, WE'VE ATTRACTED A TROOP OF SAVAGES WHOSE VICINITY DISTURBS ME.
YOU SET FOOT ON A STRANGE LAND AND YOU ARE ASTONISHED TO FIND SAVAGES? WHERE WON'T YOU FIND SAVAGES?
BESIDES, THESE CREATURES YOU CALL SAVAGES--ARE THEY WORSE THAN ANY OTHERS?
BUT, CAPTAIN, THERE ARE HUNDREDS CLIMBING ON THE PLATFORM AND THE SHIP IS STRANDED.
CALM DOWN. IF ALL THE NATIVES OF NEW GUINEA WERE ABOVE, WE'D HAVE NOTHING TO FEAR.
TOMORROW, AT 2:40, THE TIDE WILL RISE AND THE SHIP WILL BE AFLOAT.
I SLEPT POORLY, THANKS TO THE NOISE OF THE PAPUANS, WHO STAMPED ABOUT AND UTTERED DEAFENING CRIES.
BUT THE SAVAGES! WON'T THEY COME INTO THE SHIP?
THE NEXT DAY, THE CAPTAIN'S PREDICTION PROVED CORRECT. WE WERE ABOUT TO LEAVE AND ORDERS WERE GIVEN TO OPEN THE HATCHES TO RENEW OUR AIR SUPPLY.

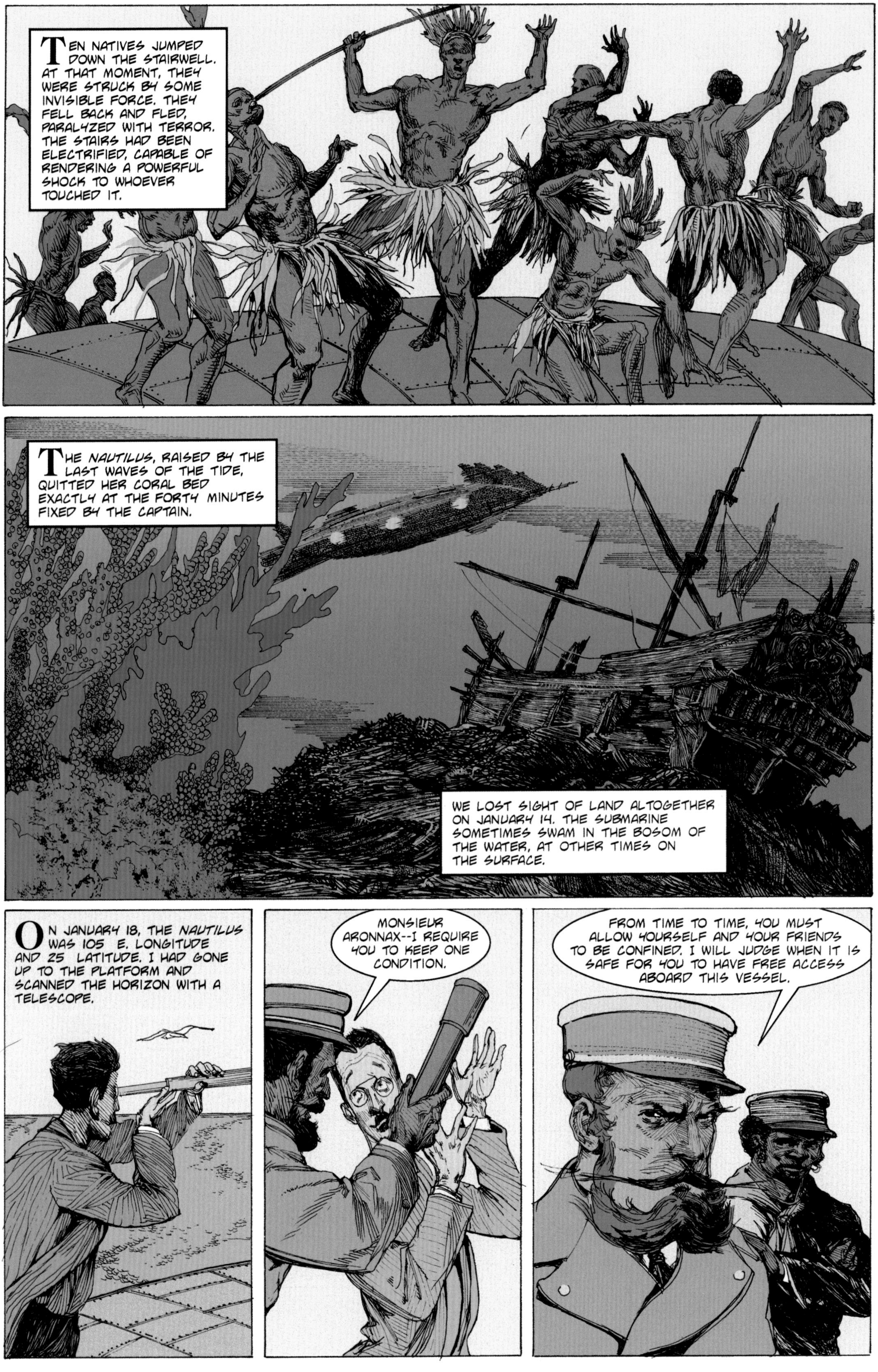
TEN NATIVES JUMPED DOWN THE STAIRWELL. AT THAT MOMENT, THEY WERE STRUCK BY SOME INVISIBLE FORCE. THEY FELL BACK AND FLED, PARALYZED WITH TERROR. THE STAIRS HAD BEEN ELECTRIFIED, CAPABLE OF RENDERING A POWERFUL SHOCK TO WHOEVER TOUCHED IT.
THE *NAUTILUS*, RAISED BY THE LAST WAVES OF THE TIDE, QUITTED HER CORAL BED EXACTLY AT THE FORTY MINUTES FIXED BY THE CAPTAIN.
WE LOST SIGHT OF LAND ALTOGETHER ON JANUARY 14. THE SUBMARINE SOMETIMES SWAM IN THE BOSOM OF THE WATER, AT OTHER TIMES ON THE SURFACE.
ON JANUARY 18, THE *NAUTILUS* WAS 105 E. LONGITUDE AND 25 LATITUDE. I HAD GONE UP TO THE PLATFORM AND SCANNED THE HORIZON WITH A TELESCOPE.
MONSIEUR ARONNAX--I REQUIRE YOU TO KEEP ONE CONDITION.
FROM TIME TO TIME, YOU MUST ALLOW YOURSELF AND YOUR FRIENDS TO BE CONFINED. I WILL JUDGE WHEN IT IS SAFE FOR YOU TO HAVE FREE ACCESS ABOARD THIS VESSEL.

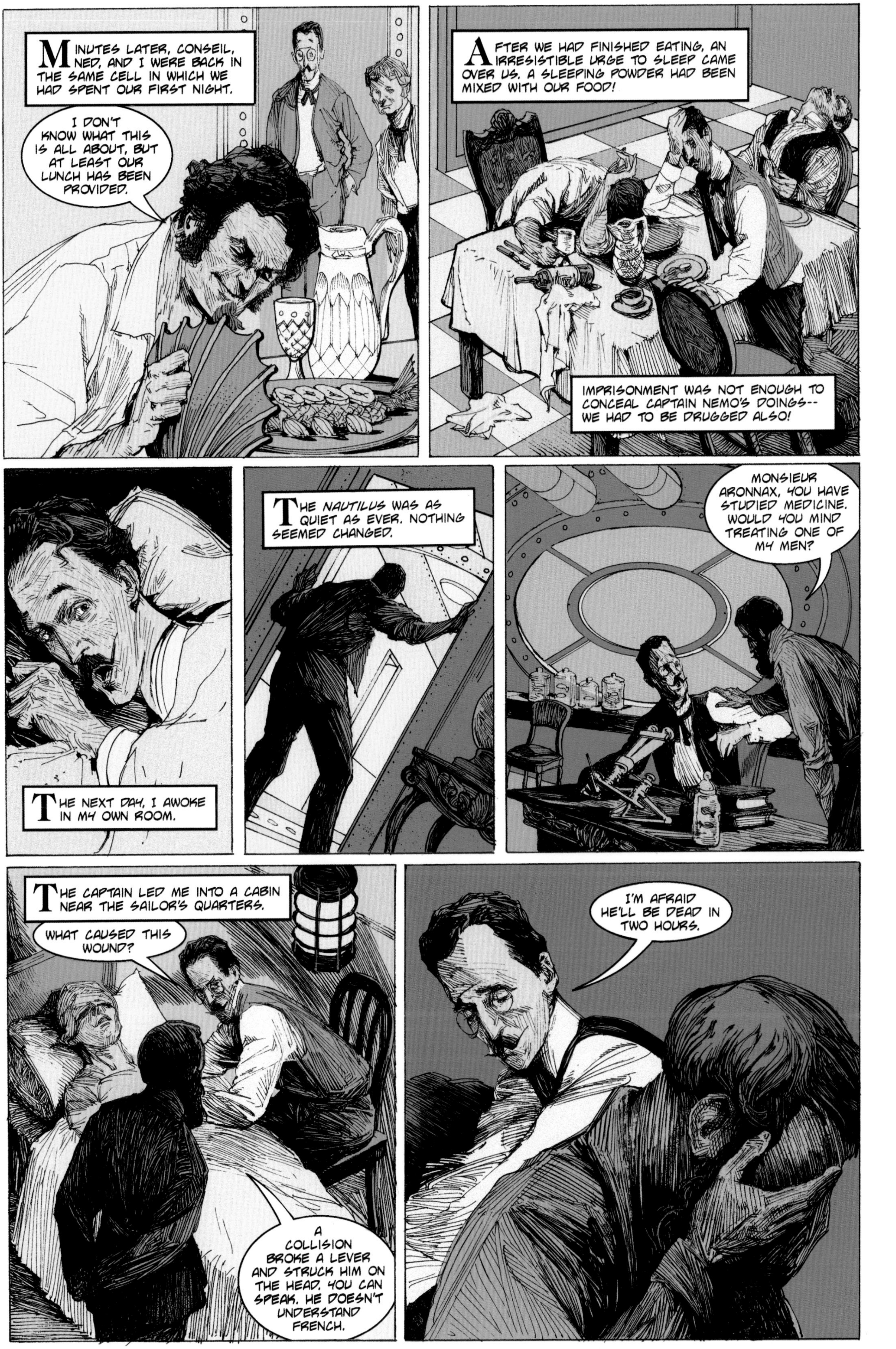
MINUTES LATER, CONSEIL, NED, AND I WERE BACK IN THE SAME CELL IN WHICH WE HAD SPENT OUR FIRST NIGHT.
I DON'T KNOW WHAT THIS IS ALL ABOUT, BUT AT LEAST OUR LUNCH HAS BEEN PROVIDED.
AFTER WE HAD FINISHED EATING, AN IRRESISTIBLE URGE TO SLEEP CAME OVER US. A SLEEPING POWDER HAD BEEN MIXED WITH OUR FOOD!
IMPRISONMENT WAS NOT ENOUGH TO CONCEAL CAPTAIN NEMO'S DOINGS-- WE HAD TO BE DRUGGED ALSO!
THE NEXT DAY, I AWOKE IN MY OWN ROOM.
THE NAUTILUS WAS AS QUIET AS EVER. NOTHING SEEMED CHANGED.
MONSIEUR ARONNAX, YOU HAVE STUDIED MEDICINE. WOULD YOU MIND TREATING ONE OF MY MEN?
THE CAPTAIN LED ME INTO A CABIN NEAR THE SAILOR'S QUARTERS.
WHAT CAUSED THIS WOUND?
A COLLISION BROKE A LEVER AND STRUCK HIM ON THE HEAD. YOU CAN SPEAK. HE DOESN'T UNDERSTAND FRENCH.
I'M AFRAID HE'LL BE DEAD IN TWO HOURS.

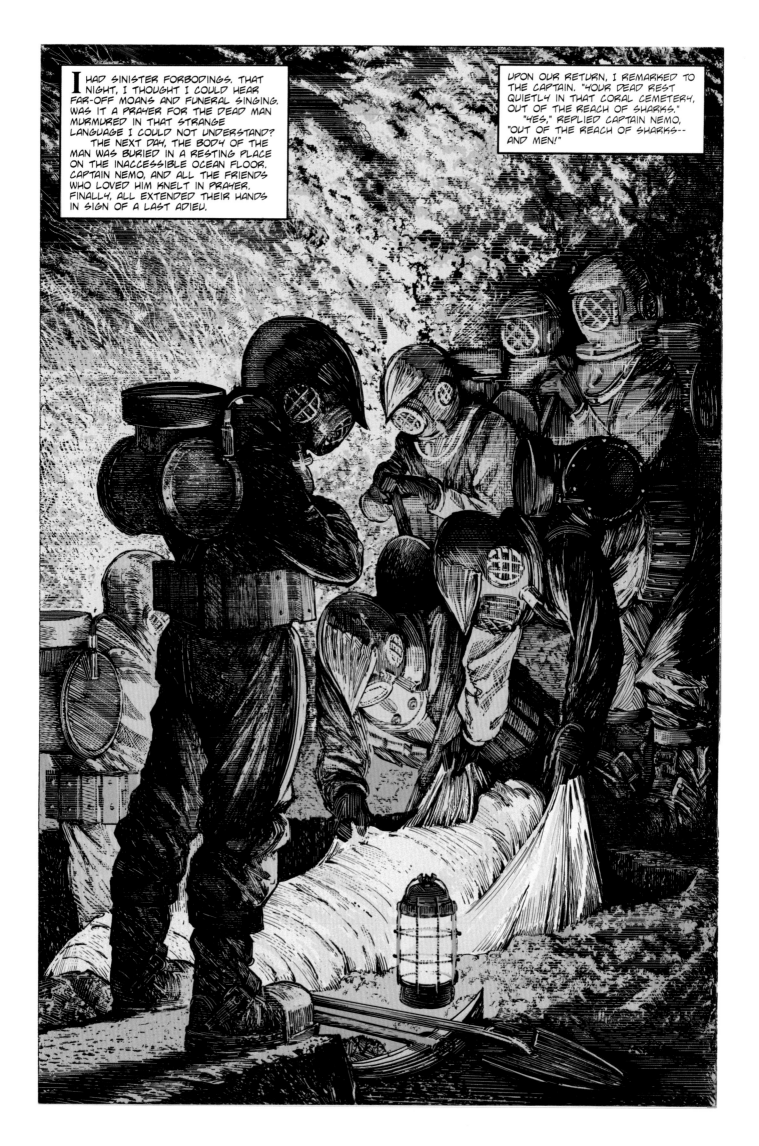

I HAD SINISTER FORBODINGS. THAT NIGHT, I THOUGHT I COULD HEAR FAR-OFF MOANS AND FUNERAL SINGING. WAS IT A PRAYER FOR THE DEAD MAN MURMURED IN THAT STRANGE LANGUAGE I COULD NOT UNDERSTAND?

THE NEXT DAY, THE BODY OF THE MAN WAS BURIED IN A RESTING PLACE ON THE INACCESSIBLE OCEAN FLOOR. CAPTAIN NEMO, AND ALL THE FRIENDS WHO LOVED HIM KNELT IN PRAYER. FINALLY, ALL EXTENDED THEIR HANDS IN SIGN OF A LAST ADIEU.

UPON OUR RETURN, I REMARKED TO THE CAPTAIN. "YOUR DEAD REST QUIETLY IN THAT CORAL CEMETERY, OUT OF THE REACH OF SHARKS."

"YES," REPLIED CAPTAIN NEMO, "OUT OF THE REACH OF SHARKS-- AND MEN!"

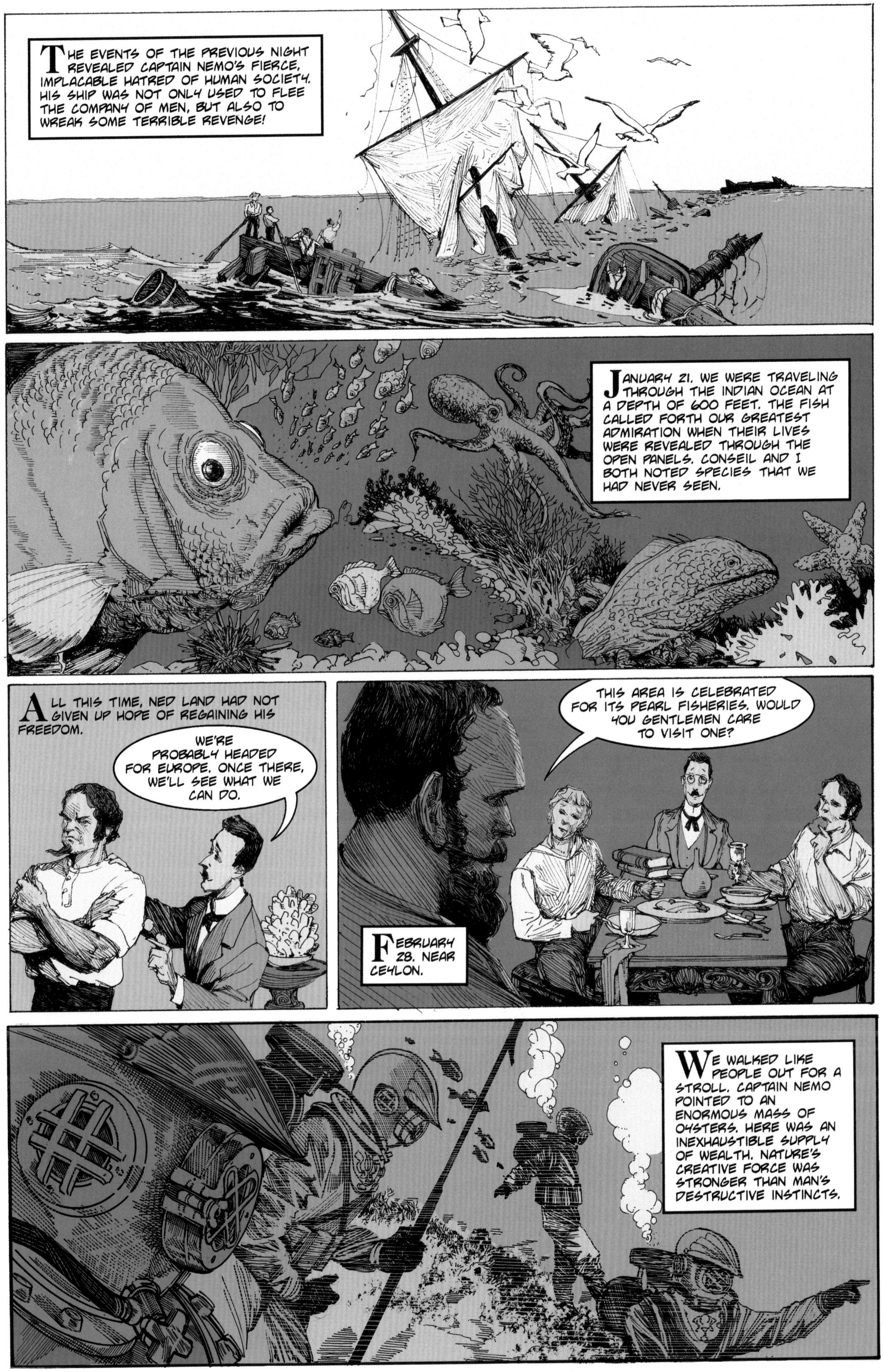
THE EVENTS OF THE PREVIOUS NIGHT REVEALED CAPTAIN NEMO'S FIERCE, IMPLACABLE HATRED OF HUMAN SOCIETY. HIS SHIP WAS NOT ONLY USED TO FLEE THE COMPANY OF MEN, BUT ALSO TO WREAK SOME TERRIBLE REVENGE!
JANUARY 21. WE WERE TRAVELING THROUGH THE INDIAN OCEAN AT A DEPTH OF 600 FEET. THE FISH CALLED FORTH OUR GREATEST ADMIRATION WHEN THEIR LIVES WERE REVEALED THROUGH THE OPEN PANELS. CONSEIL AND I BOTH NOTED SPECIES THAT WE HAD NEVER SEEN.
ALL THIS TIME, NED LAND HAD NOT GIVEN UP HOPE OF REGAINING HIS FREEDOM.
WE'RE PROBABLY HEADED FOR EUROPE. ONCE THERE, WE'LL SEE WHAT WE CAN DO.
FEBRUARY 28. NEAR CEYLON.
THIS AREA IS CELEBRATED FOR ITS PEARL FISHERIES. WOULD YOU GENTLEMEN CARE TO VISIT ONE?
WE WALKED LIKE PEOPLE OUT FOR A STROLL. CAPTAIN NEMO POINTED TO AN ENORMOUS MASS OF OYSTERS. HERE WAS AN INEXHAUSTIBLE SUPPLY OF WEALTH. NATURE'S CREATIVE FORCE WAS STRONGER THAN MAN'S DESTRUCTIVE INSTINCTS.

A SHADOW APPEARED. IT WAS A POOR DEVIL OF A FISHERMAN WHO HAD UNDOUBTEDLY COME TO GATHER WHAT HE COULD BEFORE HARVEST TIME.

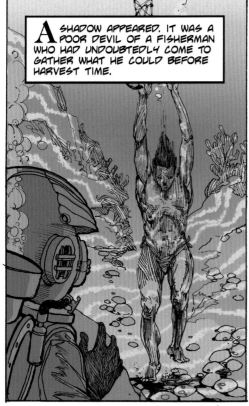

HOW COULD THIS POOR INDIAN IMAGINE THAT OTHER MEN WERE OBSERVING EVERY DETAIL OF HIS WORK?

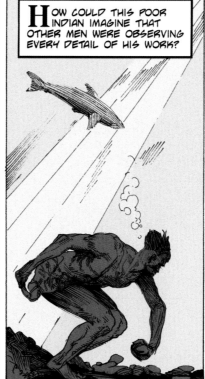

SUDDENLY, A HUGE SHARK MOVED IN AND KNOCKED THE MAN TO THE OCEAN FLOOR.

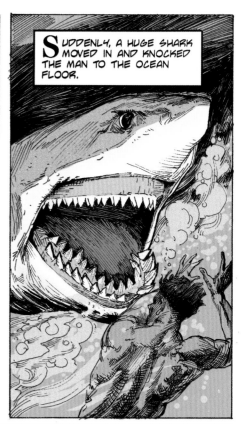

CAPTAIN NEMO JUMPED UP.

I STOOD PARALYZED AS THE CAPTAIN STRUCK MANY BLOWS, AND YET WAS UNABLE TO DELIVER A DECISIVE ONE.

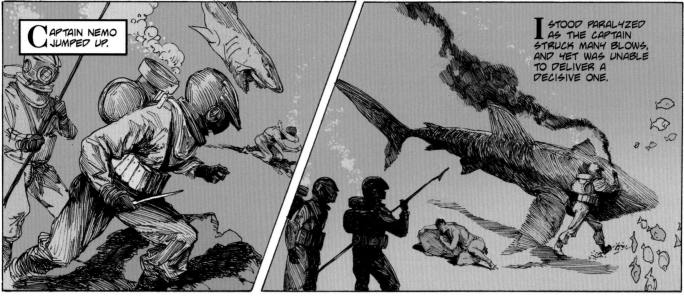

THE SHARK'S JAWS OPENED AND IT WOULD HAVE BEEN ALL OVER FOR THE CAPTAIN IF NED HAD NOT RUSHED IN...

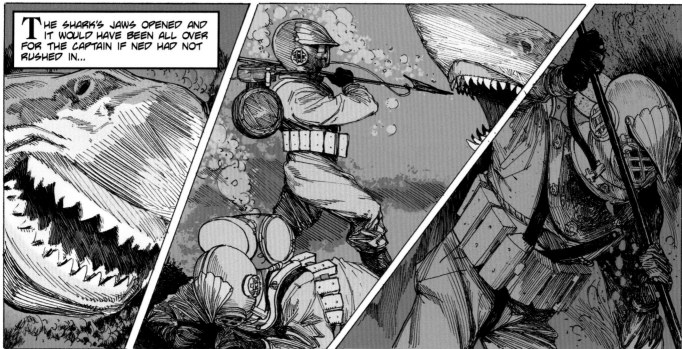

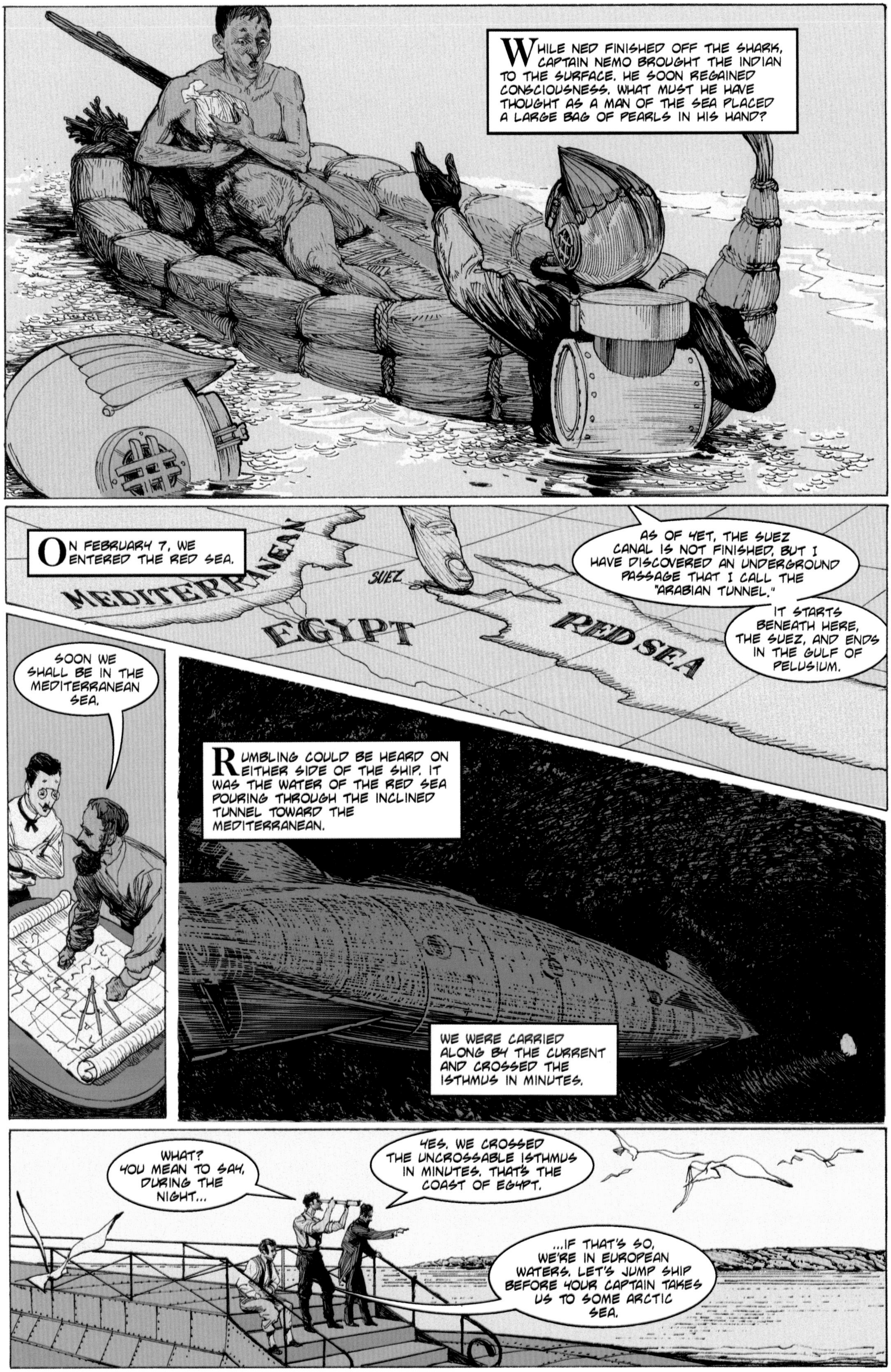
WHILE NED FINISHED OFF THE SHARK, CAPTAIN NEMO BROUGHT THE INDIAN TO THE SURFACE. HE SOON REGAINED CONSCIOUSNESS. WHAT MUST HE HAVE THOUGHT AS A MAN OF THE SEA PLACED A LARGE BAG OF PEARLS IN HIS HAND?
ON FEBRUARY 7, WE ENTERED THE RED SEA.
MEDITERRANEAN
SUEZ
EGYPT
RED SEA
AS OF YET, THE SUEZ CANAL IS NOT FINISHED, BUT I HAVE DISCOVERED AN UNDERGROUND PASSAGE THAT I CALL THE "ARABIAN TUNNEL."
IT STARTS BENEATH HERE, THE SUEZ, AND ENDS IN THE GULF OF PELUSIUM.
SOON WE SHALL BE IN THE MEDITERRANEAN SEA.
RUMBLING COULD BE HEARD ON EITHER SIDE OF THE SHIP. IT WAS THE WATER OF THE RED SEA POURING THROUGH THE INCLINED TUNNEL TOWARD THE MEDITERRANEAN.
WE WERE CARRIED ALONG BY THE CURRENT AND CROSSED THE ISTHMUS IN MINUTES.
WHAT? YOU MEAN TO SAY, DURING THE NIGHT...
YES. WE CROSSED THE UNCROSSABLE ISTHMUS IN MINUTES. THAT'S THE COAST OF EGYPT.
...IF THAT'S SO, WE'RE IN EUROPEAN WATERS. LET'S JUMP SHIP BEFORE YOUR CAPTAIN TAKES US TO SOME ARCTIC SEA.

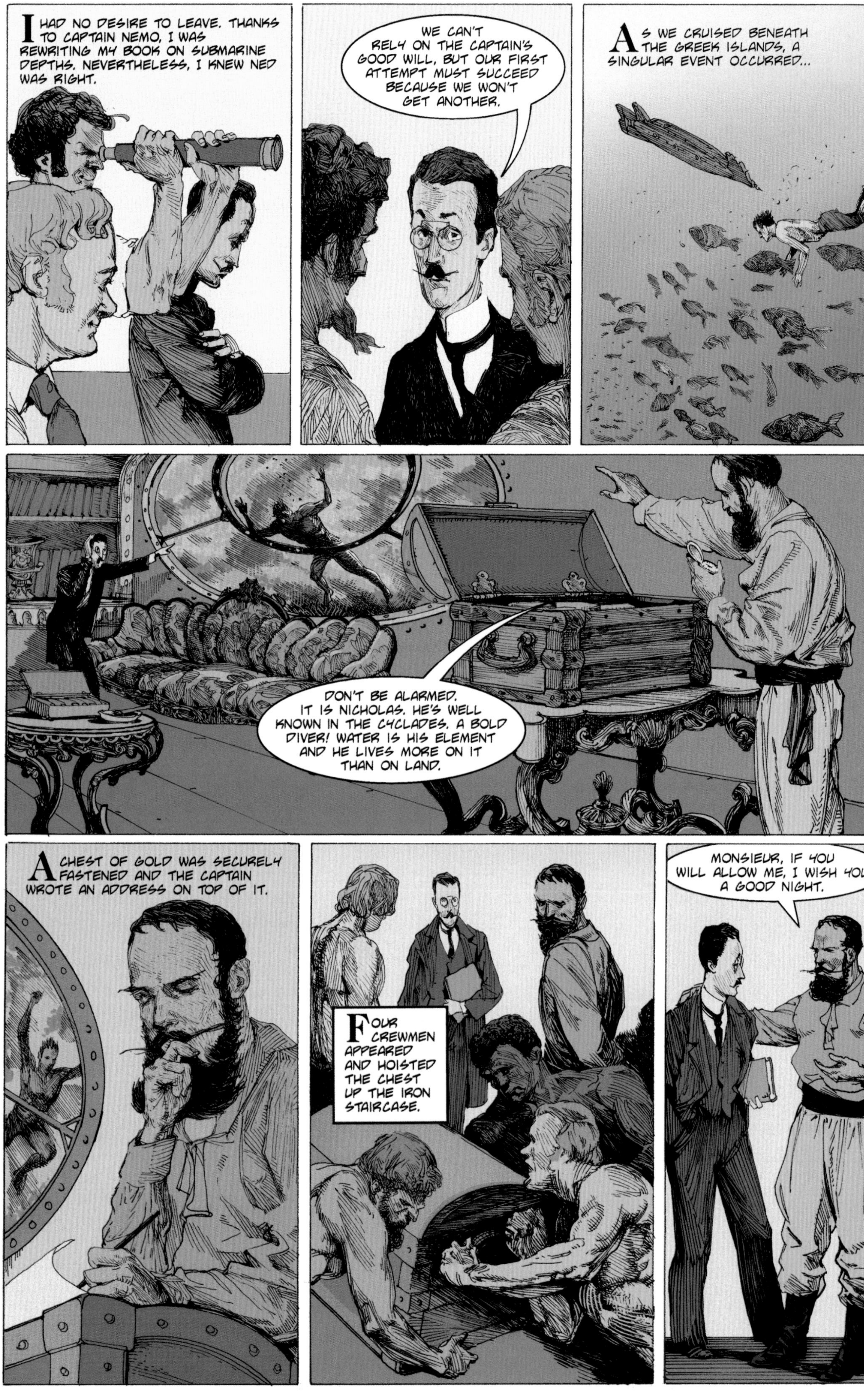
I HAD NO DESIRE TO LEAVE. THANKS TO CAPTAIN NEMO, I WAS REWRITING MY BOOK ON SUBMARINE DEPTHS. NEVERTHELESS, I KNEW NED WAS RIGHT.
WE CAN'T RELY ON THE CAPTAIN'S GOOD WILL, BUT OUR FIRST ATTEMPT MUST SUCCEED BECAUSE WE WON'T GET ANOTHER.
AS WE CRUISED BENEATH THE GREEK ISLANDS, A SINGULAR EVENT OCCURRED...
DON'T BE ALARMED. IT IS NICHOLAS. HE'S WELL KNOWN IN THE CYCLADES. A BOLD DIVER! WATER IS HIS ELEMENT AND HE LIVES MORE ON IT THAN ON LAND.
A CHEST OF GOLD WAS SECURELY FASTENED AND THE CAPTAIN WROTE AN ADDRESS ON TOP OF IT.
FOUR CREWMEN APPEARED AND HOISTED THE CHEST UP THE IRON STAIRCASE.
MONSIEUR, IF YOU WILL ALLOW ME, I WISH YOU A GOOD NIGHT.

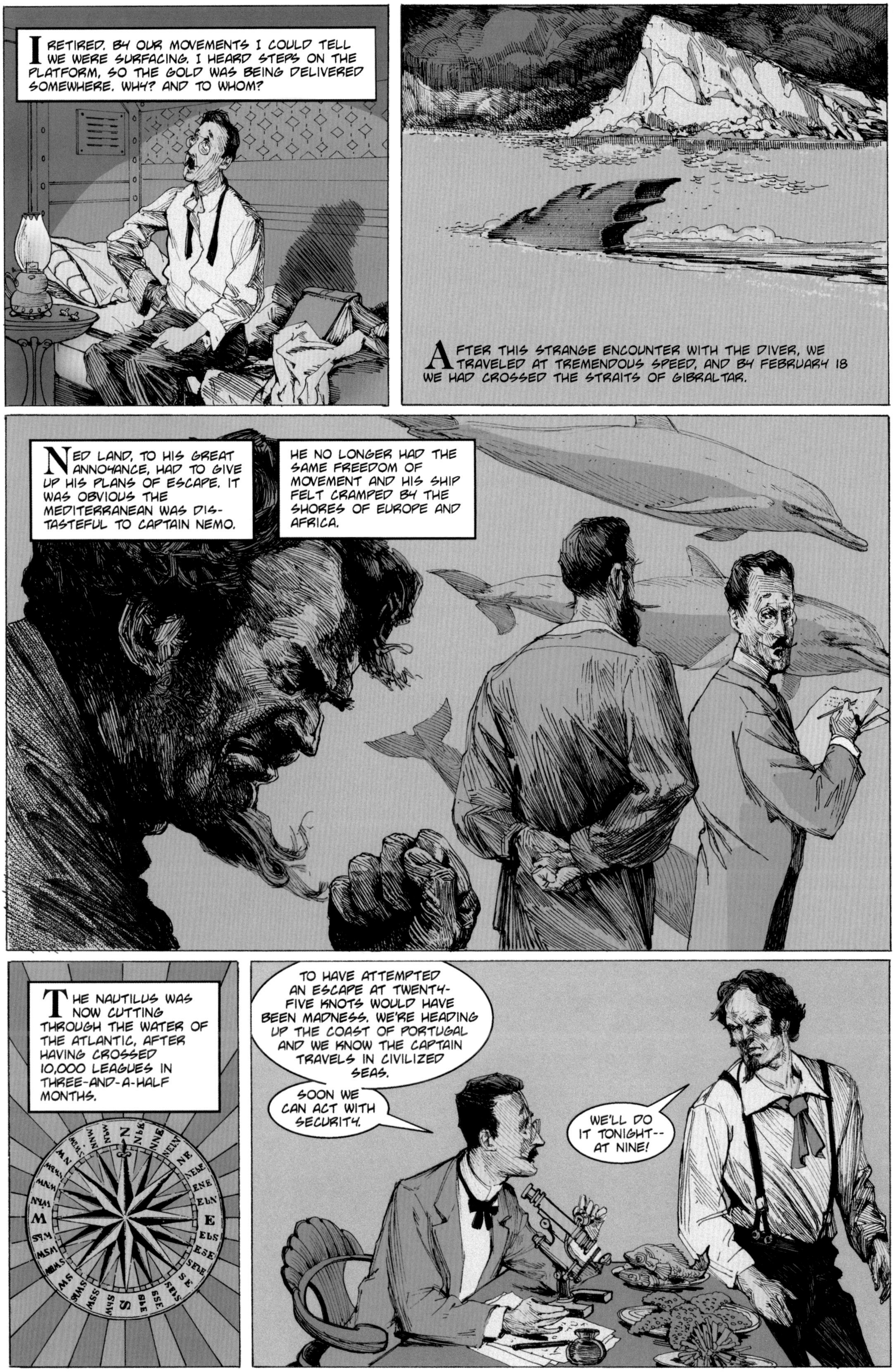
I RETIRED. BY OUR MOVEMENTS I COULD TELL WE WERE SURFACING. I HEARD STEPS ON THE PLATFORM, SO THE GOLD WAS BEING DELIVERED SOMEWHERE. WHY? AND TO WHOM?
AFTER THIS STRANGE ENCOUNTER WITH THE DIVER, WE TRAVELED AT TREMENDOUS SPEED, AND BY FEBRUARY 18 WE HAD CROSSED THE STRAITS OF GIBRALTAR.
NED LAND, TO HIS GREAT ANNOYANCE, HAD TO GIVE UP HIS PLANS OF ESCAPE. IT WAS OBVIOUS THE MEDITERRANEAN WAS DISTASTEFUL TO CAPTAIN NEMO.
HE NO LONGER HAD THE SAME FREEDOM OF MOVEMENT AND HIS SHIP FELT CRAMPED BY THE SHORES OF EUROPE AND AFRICA.
THE NAUTILUS WAS NOW CUTTING THROUGH THE WATER OF THE ATLANTIC, AFTER HAVING CROSSED 10,000 LEAGUES IN THREE-AND-A-HALF MONTHS.
TO HAVE ATTEMPTED AN ESCAPE AT TWENTY-FIVE KNOTS WOULD HAVE BEEN MADNESS. WE'RE HEADING UP THE COAST OF PORTUGAL AND WE KNOW THE CAPTAIN TRAVELS IN CIVILIZED SEAS.
SOON WE CAN ACT WITH SECURITY.
WE'LL DO IT TONIGHT--AT NINE!

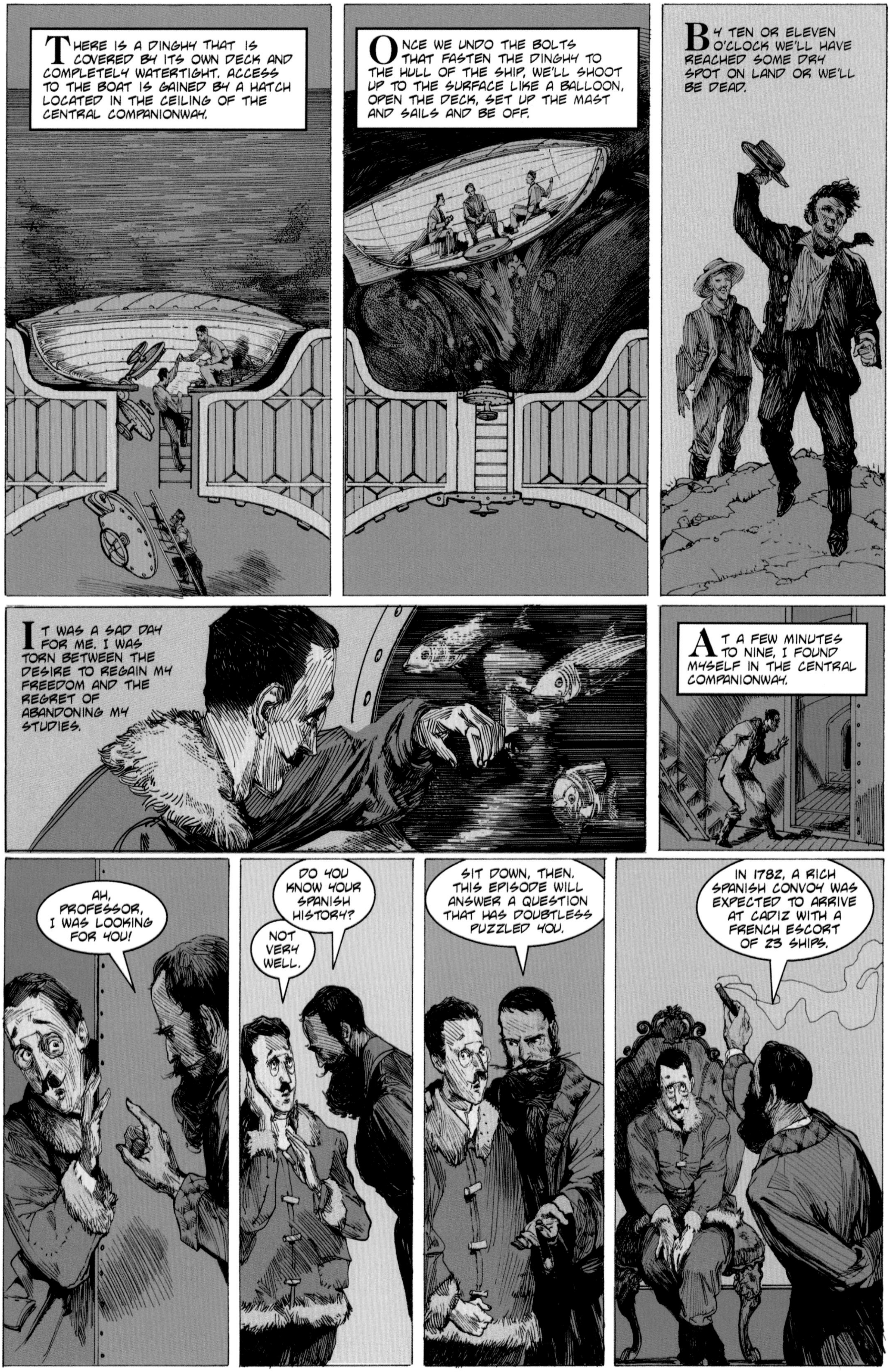
There is a dinghy that is covered by its own deck and completely watertight. Access to the boat is gained by a hatch located in the ceiling of the central companionway.
Once we undo the bolts that fasten the dinghy to the hull of the ship, we'll shoot up to the surface like a balloon, open the deck, set up the mast and sails and be off.
By ten or eleven o'clock we'll have reached some dry spot on land or we'll be dead.
It was a sad day for me. I was torn between the desire to regain my freedom and the regret of abandoning my studies.
At a few minutes to nine, I found myself in the central companionway.
Ah, professor, I was looking for you!
Do you know your Spanish history?
Not very well.
Sit down, then. This episode will answer a question that has doubtless puzzled you.
In 1782, a rich Spanish convoy was expected to arrive at Cadiz with a French escort of 23 ships.

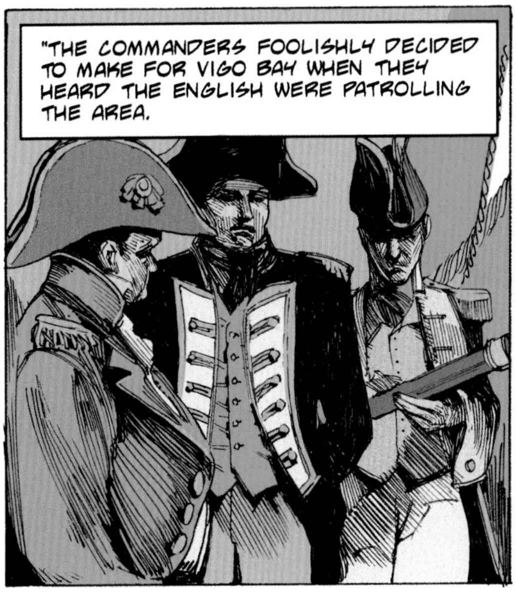
"THE COMMANDERS FOOLISHLY DECIDED TO MAKE FOR VIGO BAY WHEN THEY HEARD THE ENGLISH WERE PATROLLING THE AREA.

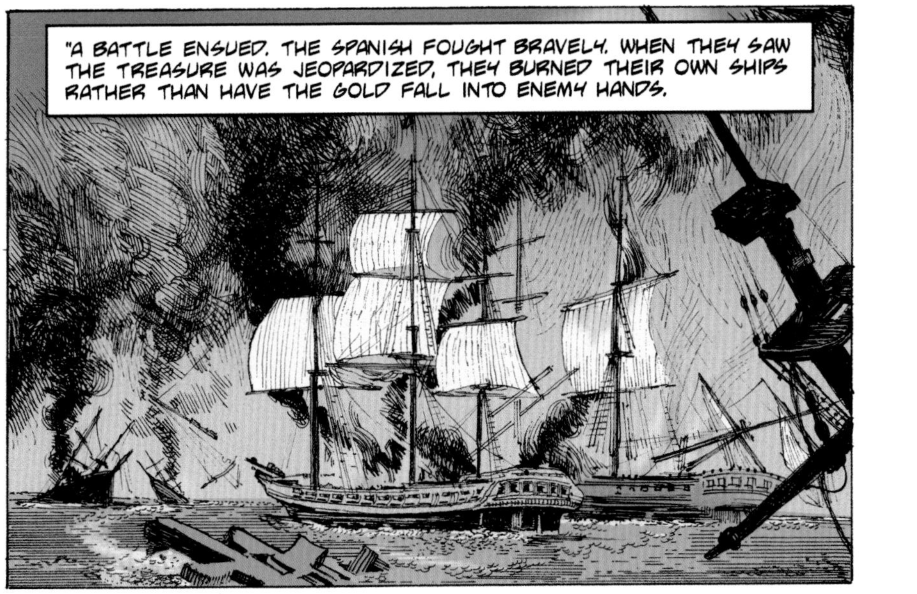
"A BATTLE ENSUED. THE SPANISH FOUGHT BRAVELY. WHEN THEY SAW THE TREASURE WAS JEOPARDIZED, THEY BURNED THEIR OWN SHIPS RATHER THAN HAVE THE GOLD FALL INTO ENEMY HANDS.

"DID YOU KNOW THAT THE SEA CONTAINED SUCH WEALTH? WHY DO YOU THINK I TAKE THE TROUBLE TO COLLECT IT?

"I MAKE GOOD USE OF IT. IT IS NOT FOR MYSELF ALONE. I AM NOT IGNORANT OF THE SUFFERING AND OPPRESSION ON THIS EARTH.

"THERE ARE MISERABLE CREATURES TO CONSOLE, VICTIMS TO AVENGE. DO YOU NOT UNDERSTAND?"

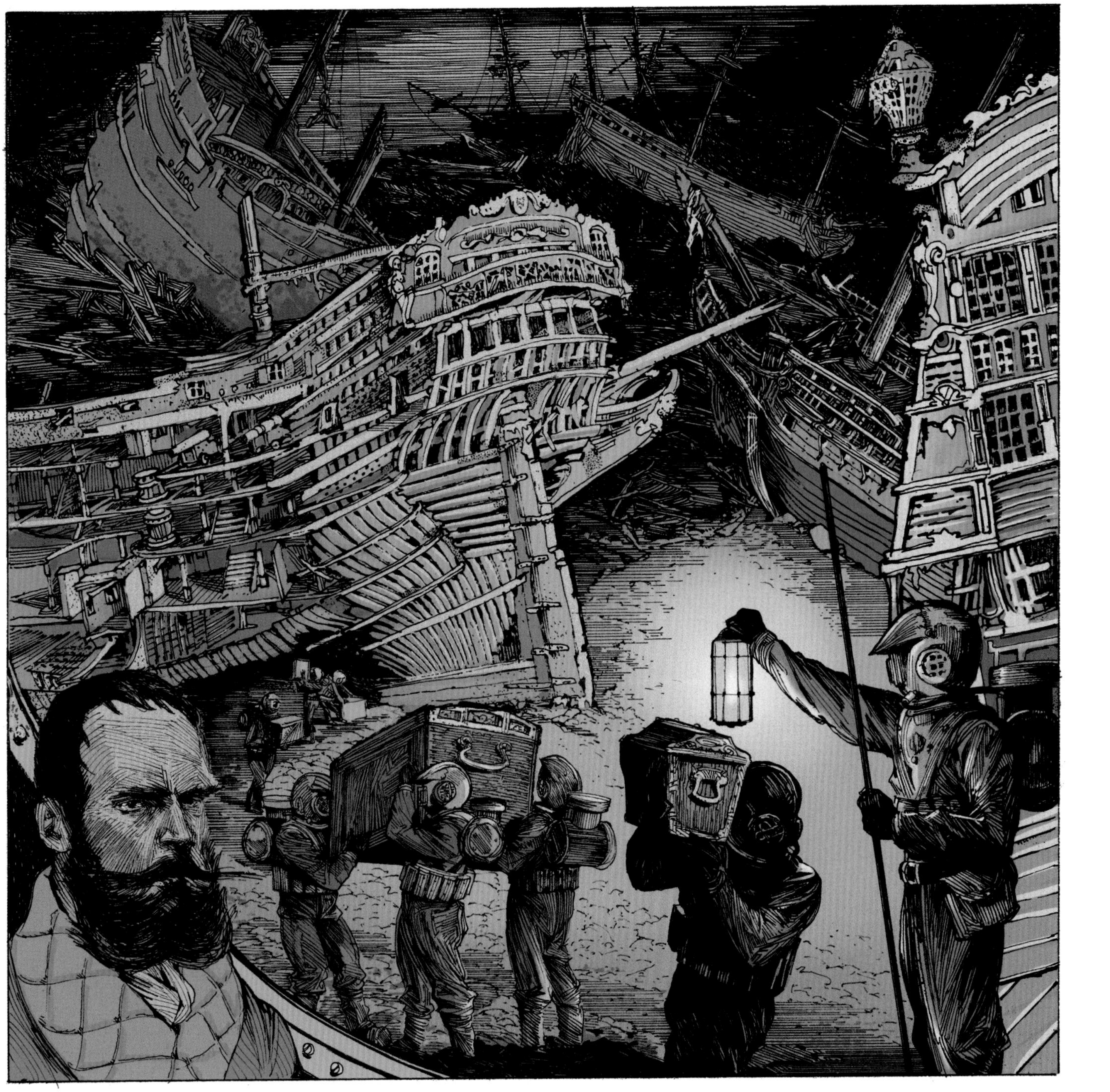

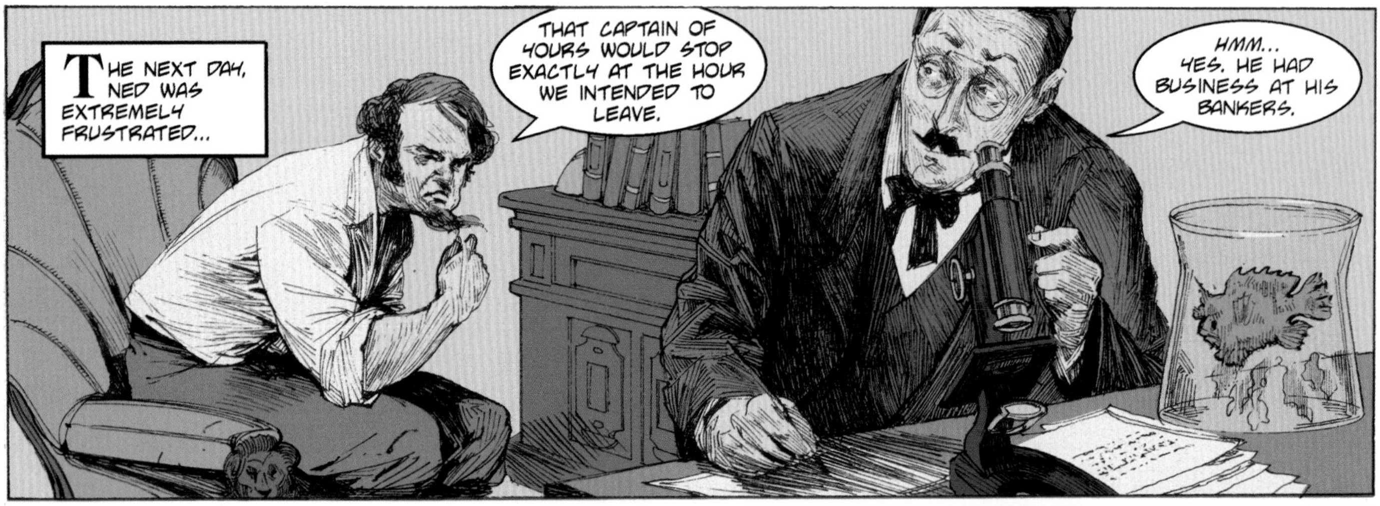
THE NEXT DAY, NED WAS EXTREMELY FRUSTRATED...
THAT CAPTAIN OF YOURS WOULD STOP EXACTLY AT THE HOUR WE INTENDED TO LEAVE.
HMM... YES. HE HAD BUSINESS AT HIS BANKERS.

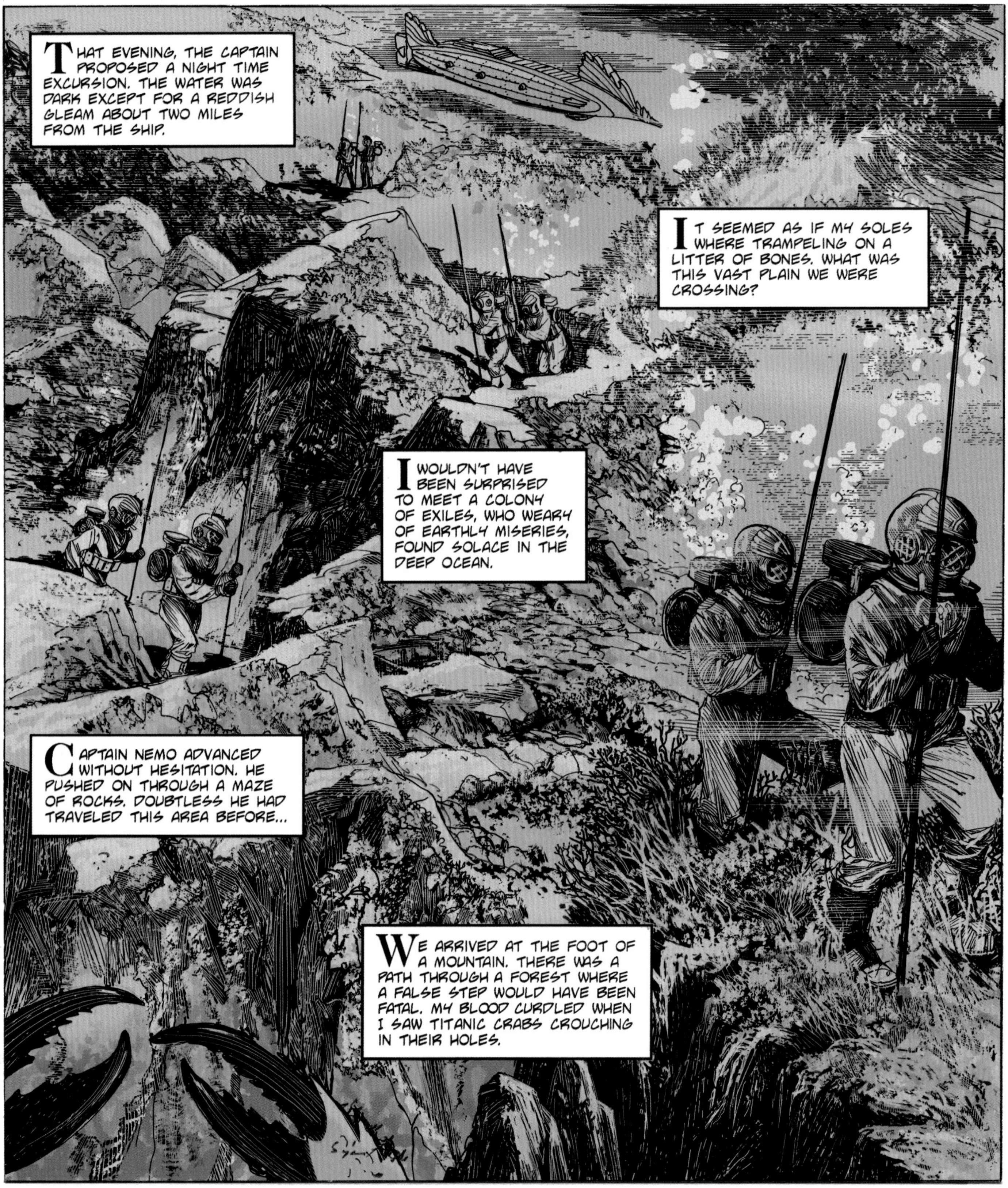
THAT EVENING, THE CAPTAIN PROPOSED A NIGHT TIME EXCURSION. THE WATER WAS DARK EXCEPT FOR A REDDISH GLEAM ABOUT TWO MILES FROM THE SHIP.
IT SEEMED AS IF MY SOLES WHERE TRAMPELING ON A LITTER OF BONES. WHAT WAS THIS VAST PLAIN WE WERE CROSSING?
I WOULDN'T HAVE BEEN SURPRISED TO MEET A COLONY OF EXILES, WHO WEARY OF EARTHLY MISERIES, FOUND SOLACE IN THE DEEP OCEAN.
CAPTAIN NEMO ADVANCED WITHOUT HESITATION. HE PUSHED ON THROUGH A MAZE OF ROCKS. DOUBTLESS HE HAD TRAVELED THIS AREA BEFORE...
WE ARRIVED AT THE FOOT OF A MOUNTAIN. THERE WAS A PATH THROUGH A FOREST WHERE A FALSE STEP WOULD HAVE BEEN FATAL. MY BLOOD CURDLED WHEN I SAW TITANIC CRABS CROUCHING IN THEIR HOLES.

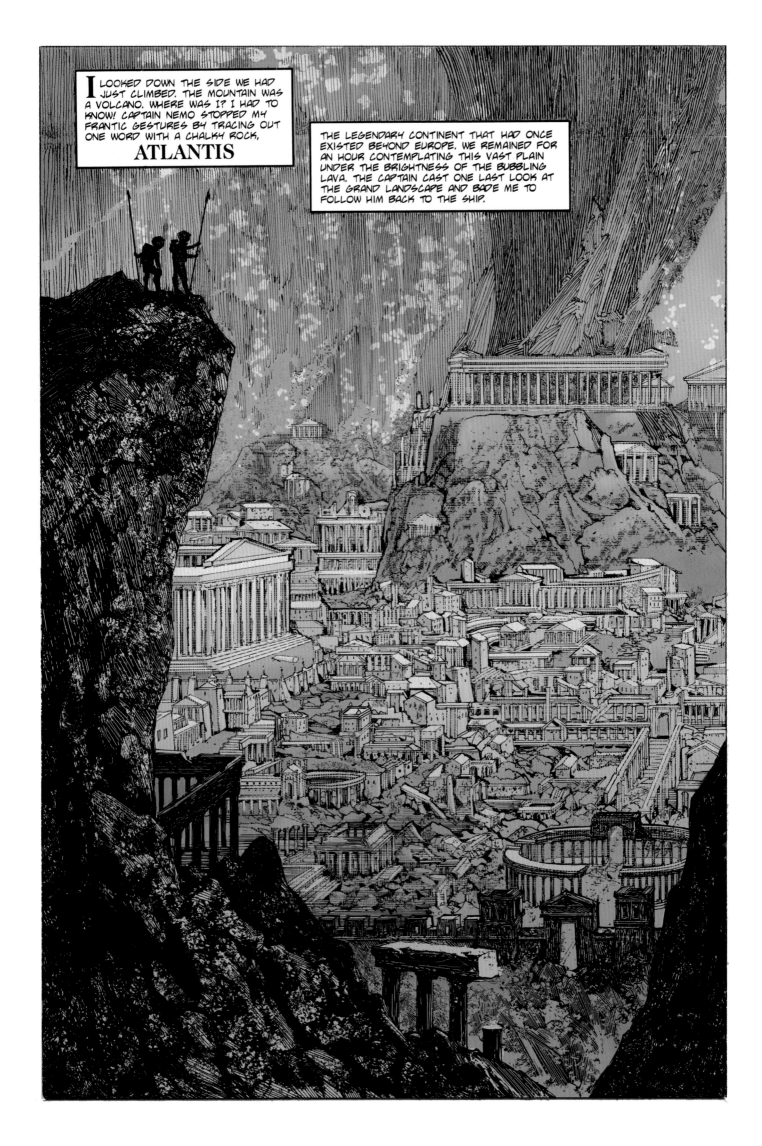

I LOOKED DOWN THE SIDE WE HAD JUST CLIMBED. THE MOUNTAIN WAS A VOLCANO. WHERE WAS I? I HAD TO KNOW! CAPTAIN NEMO STOPPED MY FRANTIC GESTURES BY TRACING OUT ONE WORD WITH A CHALKY ROCK,

ATLANTIS

THE LEGENDARY CONTINENT THAT HAD ONCE EXISTED BEYOND EUROPE. WE REMAINED FOR AN HOUR CONTEMPLATING THIS VAST PLAIN UNDER THE BRIGHTNESS OF THE BUBBLING LAVA. THE CAPTAIN CAST ONE LAST LOOK AT THE GRAND LANDSCAPE AND BADE ME TO FOLLOW HIM BACK TO THE SHIP.

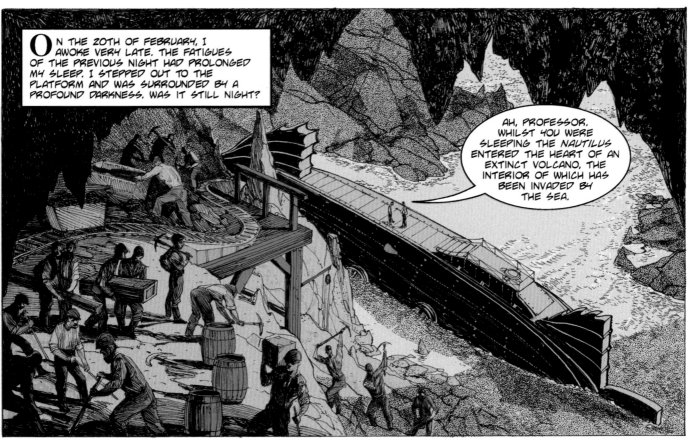

ON THE 20TH OF FEBRUARY, I AWOKE VERY LATE. THE FATIGUES OF THE PREVIOUS NIGHT HAD PROLONGED MY SLEEP. I STEPPED OUT TO THE PLATFORM AND WAS SURROUNDED BY A PROFOUND DARKNESS. WAS IT STILL NIGHT?

AH, PROFESSOR. WHILST YOU WERE SLEEPING THE NAUTILUS ENTERED THE HEART OF AN EXTINCT VOLCANO, THE INTERIOR OF WHICH HAS BEEN INVADED BY THE SEA.

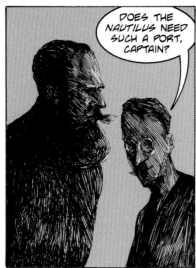

DOES THE NAUTILUS NEED SUCH A PORT, CAPTAIN?

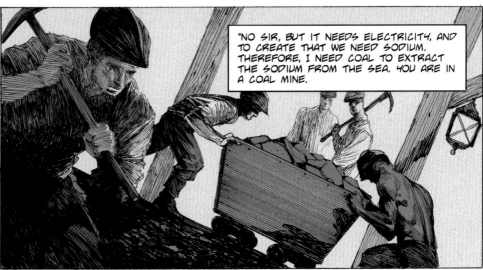

"NO SIR, BUT IT NEEDS ELECTRICITY, AND TO CREATE THAT WE NEED SODIUM. THEREFORE, I NEED COAL TO EXTRACT THE SODIUM FROM THE SEA. YOU ARE IN A COAL MINE."

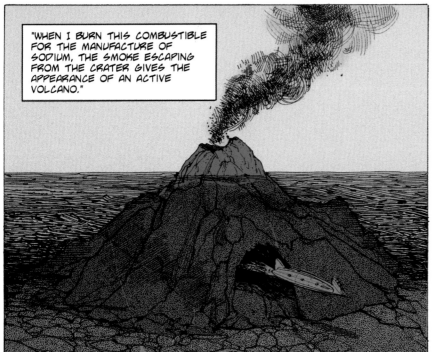

"WHEN I BURN THIS COMBUSTIBLE FOR THE MANUFACTURE OF SODIUM, THE SMOKE ESCAPING FROM THE CRATER GIVES THE APPEARANCE OF AN ACTIVE VOLCANO."

FOR NINETEEN DAYS THE NAUTILUS STEERED SOUTH. I HAD NO DOUBTS THAT AFTER GOING AROUND CAPE HORN WE'D TURN WEST, BUT THE SHIP DID NOTHING OF THE SORT AND MERELY CONTINUED IN THE DIRECTION OF THE ANTARCTIC.

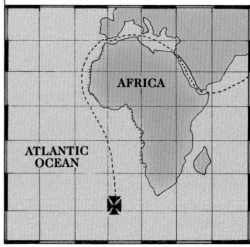

AFRICA

ATLANTIC OCEAN

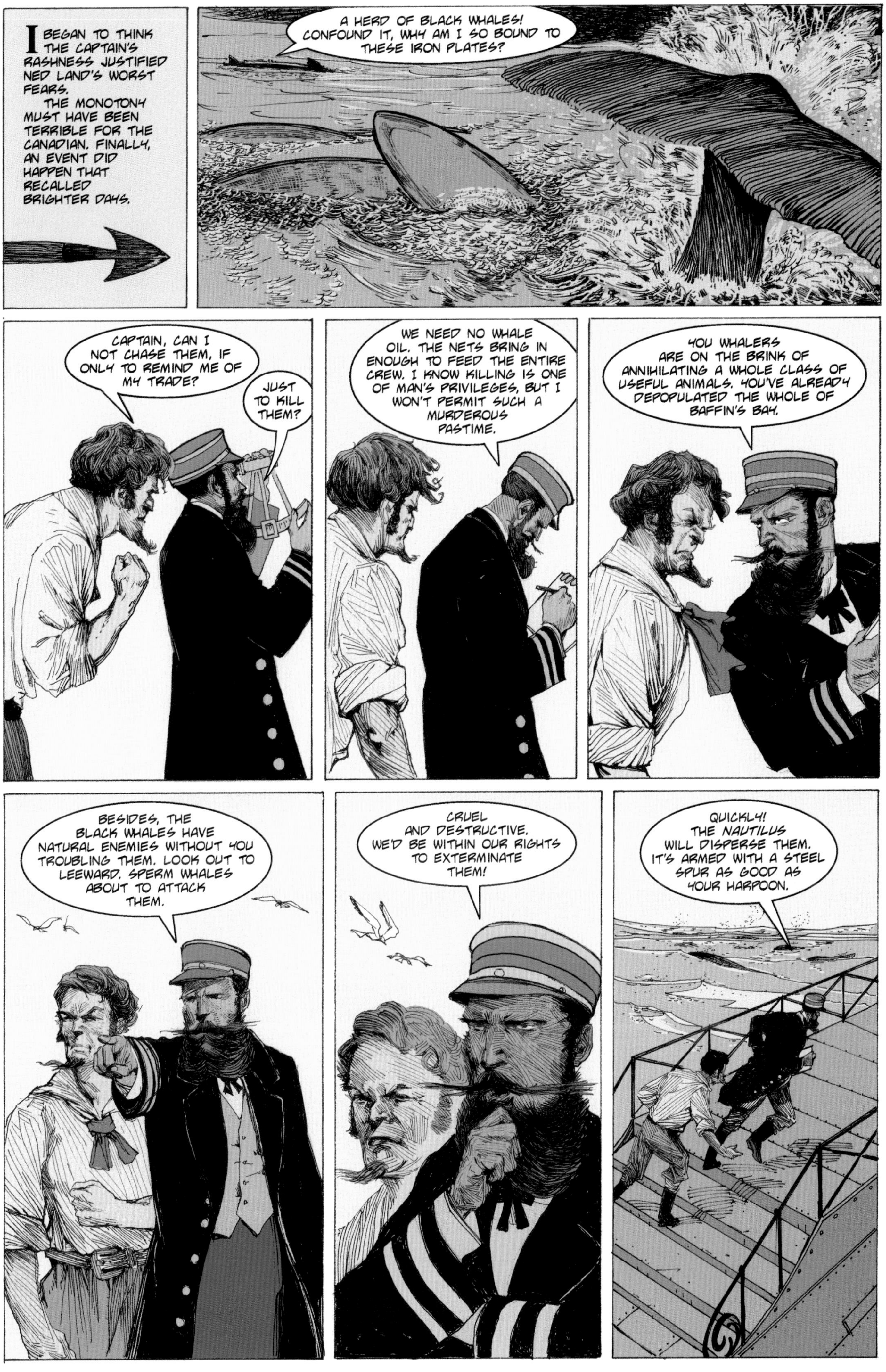
I BEGAN TO THINK THE CAPTAIN'S RASHNESS JUSTIFIED NED LAND'S WORST FEARS.
THE MONOTONY MUST HAVE BEEN TERRIBLE FOR THE CANADIAN. FINALLY, AN EVENT DID HAPPEN THAT RECALLED BRIGHTER DAYS.
A HERD OF BLACK WHALES! CONFOUND IT, WHY AM I SO BOUND TO THESE IRON PLATES?
CAPTAIN, CAN I NOT CHASE THEM, IF ONLY TO REMIND ME OF MY TRADE?
JUST TO KILL THEM?
WE NEED NO WHALE OIL. THE NETS BRING IN ENOUGH TO FEED THE ENTIRE CREW. I KNOW KILLING IS ONE OF MAN'S PRIVILEGES, BUT I WON'T PERMIT SUCH A MURDEROUS PASTIME.
YOU WHALERS ARE ON THE BRINK OF ANNIHILATING A WHOLE CLASS OF USEFUL ANIMALS. YOU'VE ALREADY DEPOPULATED THE WHOLE OF BAFFIN'S BAY.
BESIDES, THE BLACK WHALES HAVE NATURAL ENEMIES WITHOUT YOU TROUBLING THEM. LOOK OUT TO LEEWARD. SPERM WHALES ABOUT TO ATTACK THEM.
CRUEL AND DESTRUCTIVE. WE'D BE WITHIN OUR RIGHTS TO EXTERMINATE THEM!
QUICKLY! THE *NAUTILUS* WILL DISPERSE THEM. IT'S ARMED WITH A STEEL SPUR AS GOOD AS YOUR HARPOON.

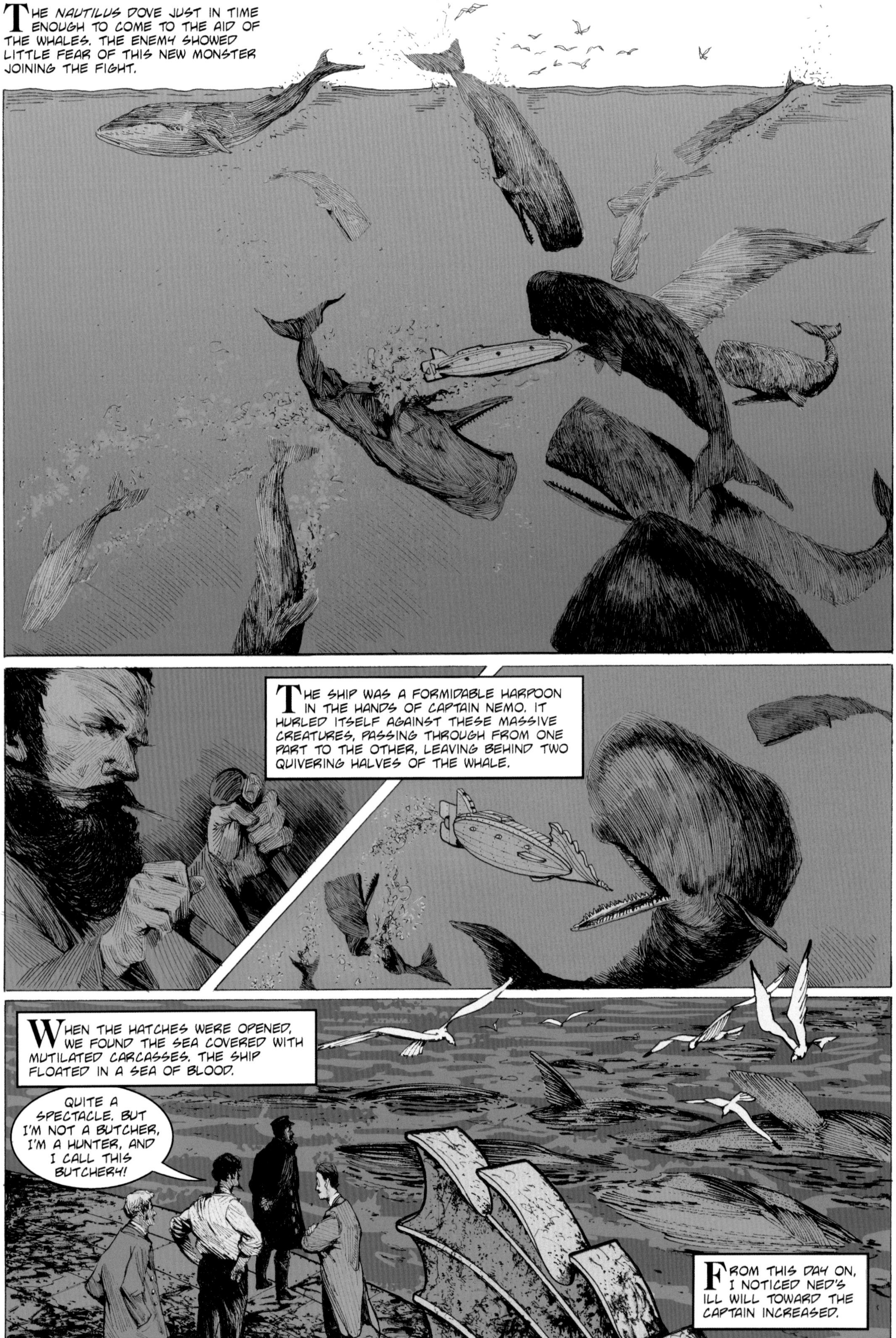
THE *NAUTILUS* DOVE JUST IN TIME ENOUGH TO COME TO THE AID OF THE WHALES. THE ENEMY SHOWED LITTLE FEAR OF THIS NEW MONSTER JOINING THE FIGHT.
THE SHIP WAS A FORMIDABLE HARPOON IN THE HANDS OF CAPTAIN NEMO. IT HURLED ITSELF AGAINST THESE MASSIVE CREATURES, PASSING THROUGH FROM ONE PART TO THE OTHER, LEAVING BEHIND TWO QUIVERING HALVES OF THE WHALE.
WHEN THE HATCHES WERE OPENED, WE FOUND THE SEA COVERED WITH MUTILATED CARCASSES. THE SHIP FLOATED IN A SEA OF BLOOD.
QUITE A SPECTACLE. BUT I'M NOT A BUTCHER, I'M A HUNTER, AND I CALL THIS BUTCHERY!
FROM THIS DAY ON, I NOTICED NED'S ILL WILL TOWARD THE CAPTAIN INCREASED.

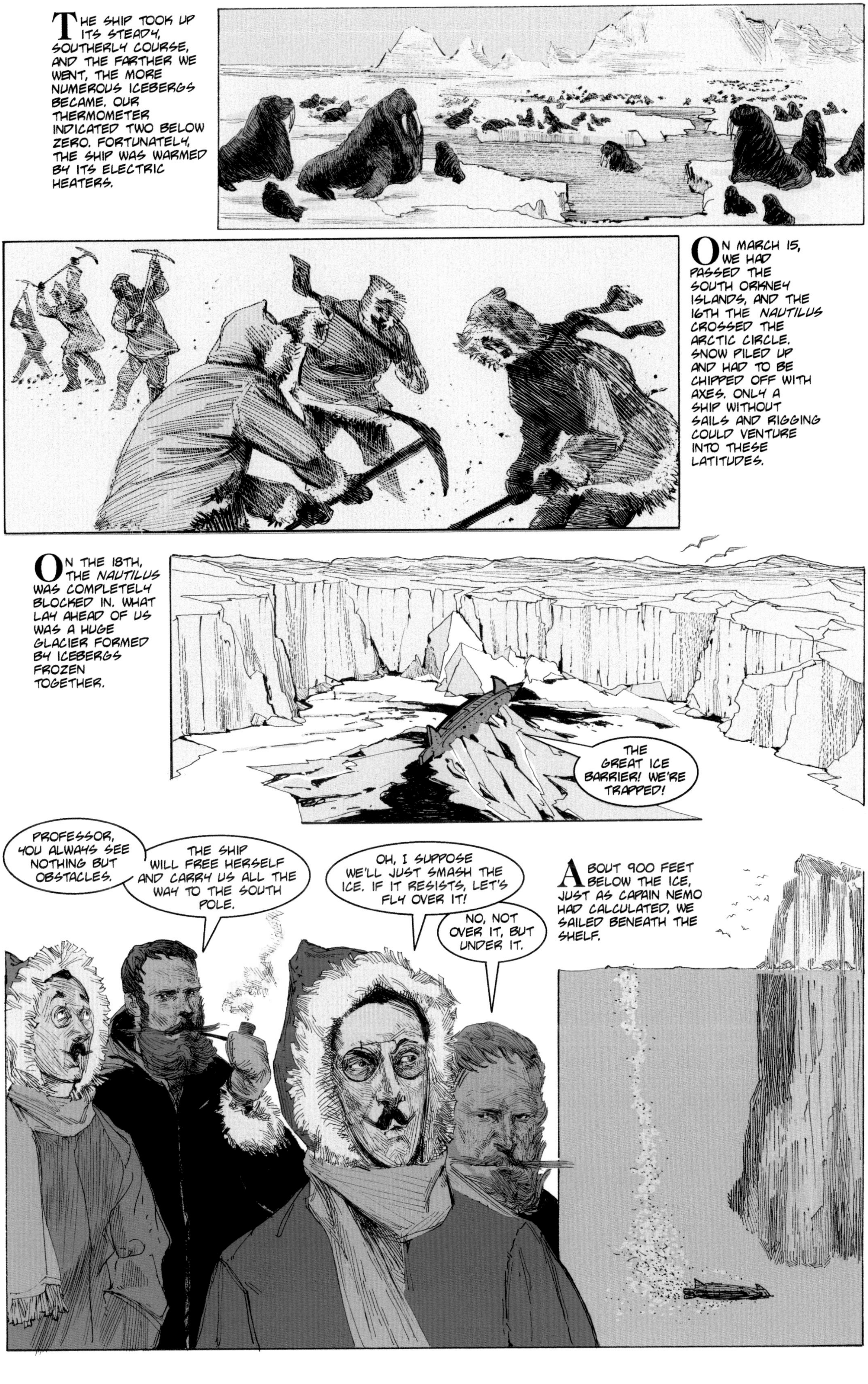
THE SHIP TOOK UP ITS STEADY, SOUTHERLY COURSE, AND THE FARTHER WE WENT, THE MORE NUMEROUS ICEBERGS BECAME. OUR THERMOMETER INDICATED TWO BELOW ZERO. FORTUNATELY, THE SHIP WAS WARMED BY ITS ELECTRIC HEATERS.
ON MARCH 15, WE HAD PASSED THE SOUTH ORKNEY ISLANDS, AND THE 16TH THE *NAUTILUS* CROSSED THE ARCTIC CIRCLE. SNOW PILED UP AND HAD TO BE CHIPPED OFF WITH AXES. ONLY A SHIP WITHOUT SAILS AND RIGGING COULD VENTURE INTO THESE LATITUDES.
ON THE 18TH, THE *NAUTILUS* WAS COMPLETELY BLOCKED IN. WHAT LAY AHEAD OF US WAS A HUGE GLACIER FORMED BY ICEBERGS FROZEN TOGETHER.
THE GREAT ICE BARRIER! WE'RE TRAPPED!
PROFESSOR, YOU ALWAYS SEE NOTHING BUT OBSTACLES.
THE SHIP WILL FREE HERSELF AND CARRY US ALL THE WAY TO THE SOUTH POLE.
OH, I SUPPOSE WE'LL JUST SMASH THE ICE. IF IT RESISTS, LET'S FLY OVER IT!
NO, NOT OVER IT, BUT UNDER IT.
ABOUT 900 FEET BELOW THE ICE, JUST AS CAPAIN NEMO HAD CALCULATED, WE SAILED BENEATH THE SHELF.

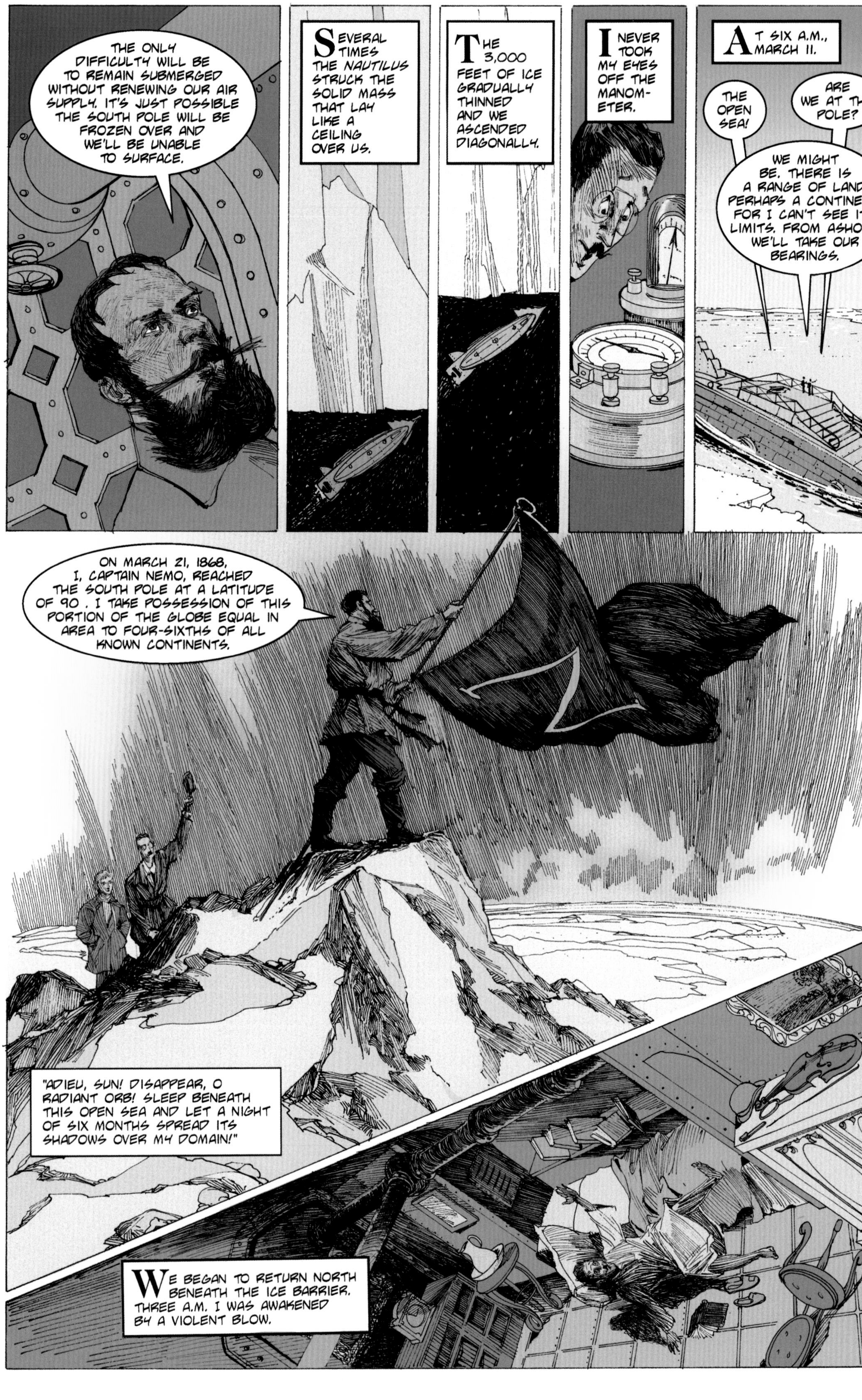
THE ONLY DIFFICULTY WILL BE TO REMAIN SUBMERGED WITHOUT RENEWING OUR AIR SUPPLY. IT'S JUST POSSIBLE THE SOUTH POLE WILL BE FROZEN OVER AND WE'LL BE UNABLE TO SURFACE.
SEVERAL TIMES THE NAUTILUS STRUCK THE SOLID MASS THAT LAY LIKE A CEILING OVER US.
THE 3,000 FEET OF ICE GRADUALLY THINNED AND WE ASCENDED DIAGONALLY.
I NEVER TOOK MY EYES OFF THE MANOMETER.
AT SIX A.M., MARCH 11.
THE OPEN SEA!
ARE WE AT THE POLE?
WE MIGHT BE. THERE IS A RANGE OF LAND, PERHAPS A CONTINENT, FOR I CAN'T SEE ITS LIMITS. FROM ASHORE WE'LL TAKE OUR BEARINGS.
ON MARCH 21, 1868, I, CAPTAIN NEMO, REACHED THE SOUTH POLE AT A LATITUDE OF 90 . I TAKE POSSESSION OF THIS PORTION OF THE GLOBE EQUAL IN AREA TO FOUR-SIXTHS OF ALL KNOWN CONTINENTS.
"ADIEU, SUN! DISAPPEAR, O RADIANT ORB! SLEEP BENEATH THIS OPEN SEA AND LET A NIGHT OF SIX MONTHS SPREAD ITS SHADOWS OVER MY DOMAIN!"
WE BEGAN TO RETURN NORTH BENEATH THE ICE BARRIER. THREE A.M. I WAS AWAKENED BY A VIOLENT BLOW.

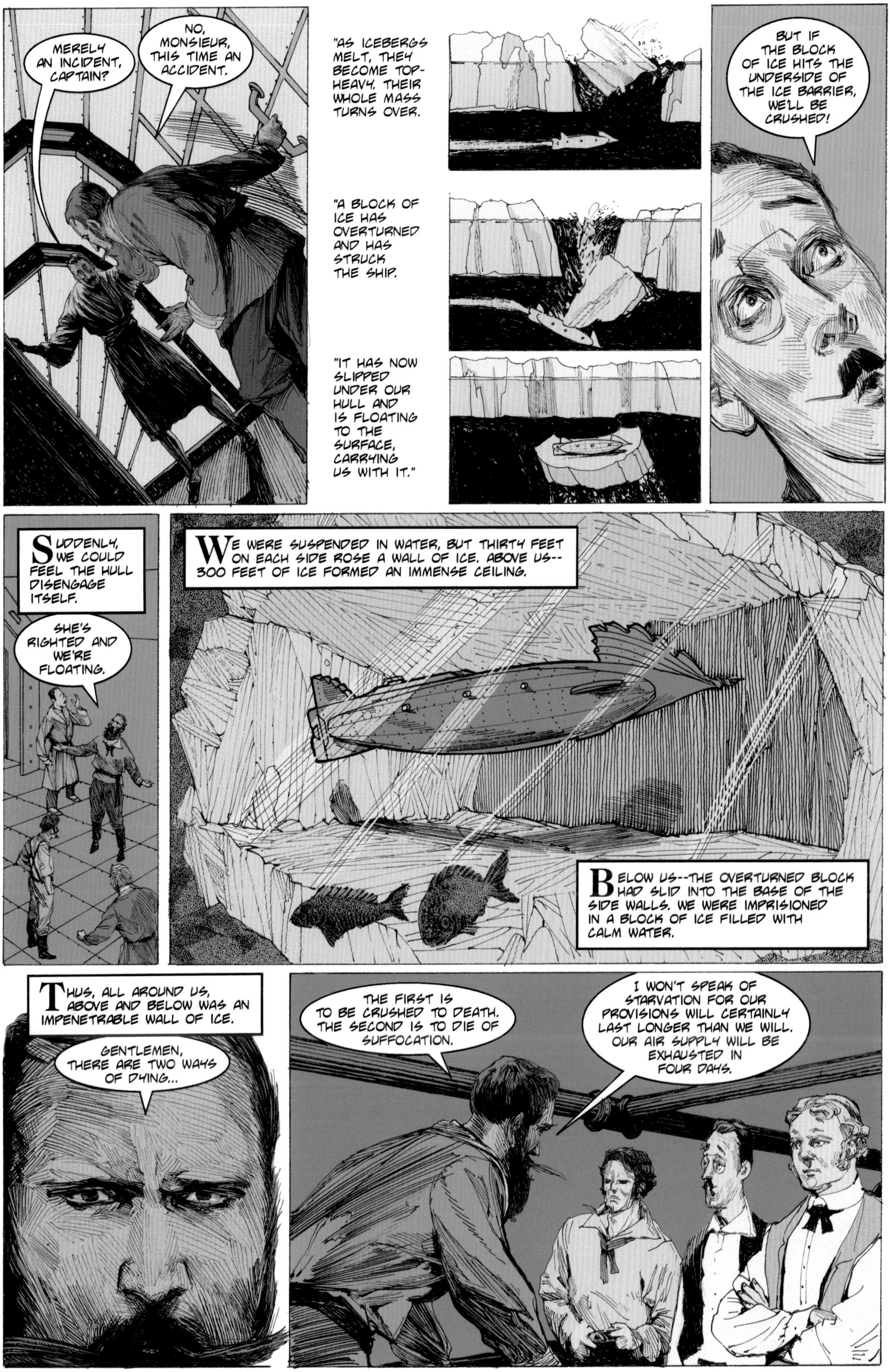
MERELY AN INCIDENT, CAPTAIN?
NO, MONSIEUR, THIS TIME AN ACCIDENT.
"AS ICEBERGS MELT, THEY BECOME TOP-HEAVY. THEIR WHOLE MASS TURNS OVER.
"A BLOCK OF ICE HAS OVERTURNED AND HAS STRUCK THE SHIP.
"IT HAS NOW SLIPPED UNDER OUR HULL AND IS FLOATING TO THE SURFACE, CARRYING US WITH IT."
BUT IF THE BLOCK OF ICE HITS THE UNDERSIDE OF THE ICE BARRIER, WE'LL BE CRUSHED!
SUDDENLY, WE COULD FEEL THE HULL DISENGAGE ITSELF.
SHE'S RIGHTED AND WE'RE FLOATING.
WE WERE SUSPENDED IN WATER, BUT THIRTY FEET ON EACH SIDE ROSE A WALL OF ICE. ABOVE US--300 FEET OF ICE FORMED AN IMMENSE CEILING.
BELOW US--THE OVERTURNED BLOCK HAD SLID INTO THE BASE OF THE SIDE WALLS. WE WERE IMPRISIONED IN A BLOCK OF ICE FILLED WITH CALM WATER.
THUS, ALL AROUND US, ABOVE AND BELOW WAS AN IMPENETRABLE WALL OF ICE.
GENTLEMEN, THERE ARE TWO WAYS OF DYING...
THE FIRST IS TO BE CRUSHED TO DEATH. THE SECOND IS TO DIE OF SUFFOCATION.
I WON'T SPEAK OF STARVATION FOR OUR PROVISIONS WILL CERTAINLY LAST LONGER THAN WE WILL. OUR AIR SUPPLY WILL BE EXHAUSTED IN FOUR DAYS.

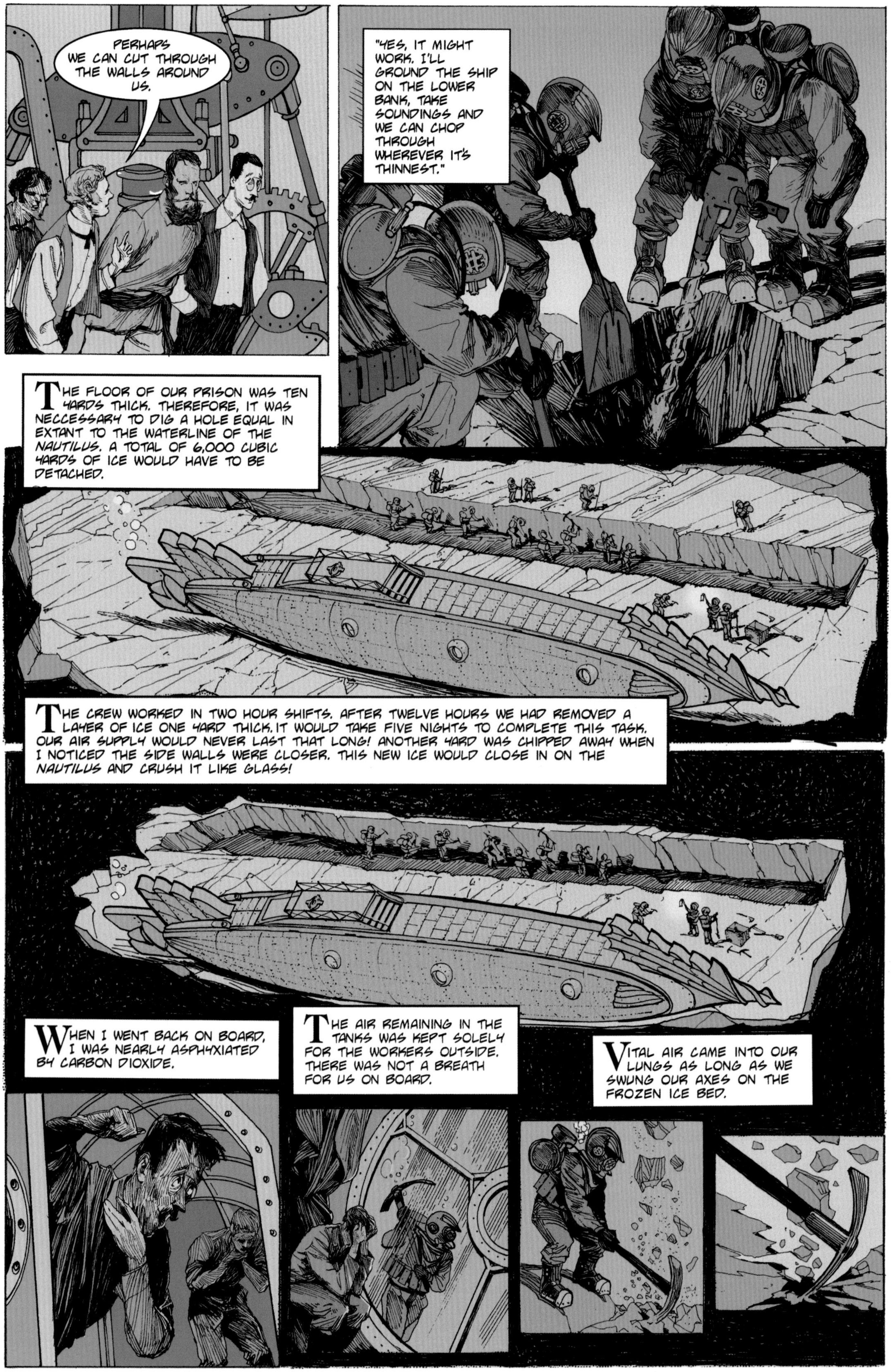
PERHAPS WE CAN CUT THROUGH THE WALLS AROUND US.
"YES, IT MIGHT WORK. I'LL GROUND THE SHIP ON THE LOWER BANK, TAKE SOUNDINGS AND WE CAN CHOP THROUGH WHEREVER IT'S THINNEST."
THE FLOOR OF OUR PRISON WAS TEN YARDS THICK. THEREFORE, IT WAS NECCESSARY TO DIG A HOLE EQUAL IN EXTANT TO THE WATERLINE OF THE NAUTILUS. A TOTAL OF 6,000 CUBIC YARDS OF ICE WOULD HAVE TO BE DETACHED.
THE CREW WORKED IN TWO HOUR SHIFTS. AFTER TWELVE HOURS WE HAD REMOVED A LAYER OF ICE ONE YARD THICK. IT WOULD TAKE FIVE NIGHTS TO COMPLETE THIS TASK. OUR AIR SUPPLY WOULD NEVER LAST THAT LONG! ANOTHER YARD WAS CHIPPED AWAY WHEN I NOTICED THE SIDE WALLS WERE CLOSER. THIS NEW ICE WOULD CLOSE IN ON THE NAUTILUS AND CRUSH IT LIKE GLASS!
WHEN I WENT BACK ON BOARD, I WAS NEARLY ASPHYXIATED BY CARBON DIOXIDE.
THE AIR REMAINING IN THE TANKS WAS KEPT SOLELY FOR THE WORKERS OUTSIDE. THERE WAS NOT A BREATH FOR US ON BOARD.
VITAL AIR CAME INTO OUR LUNGS AS LONG AS WE SWUNG OUR AXES ON THE FROZEN ICE BED.

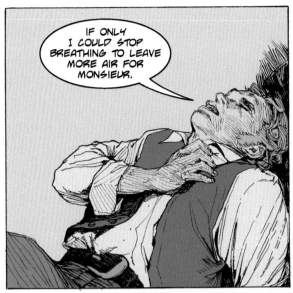

IF ONLY I COULD STOP BREATHING TO LEAVE MORE AIR FOR MONSIEUR.

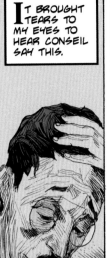

It BROUGHT TEARS TO MY EYES TO HEAR CONSEIL SAY THIS.

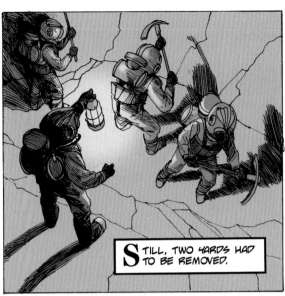

Still, TWO YARDS HAD TO BE REMOVED.

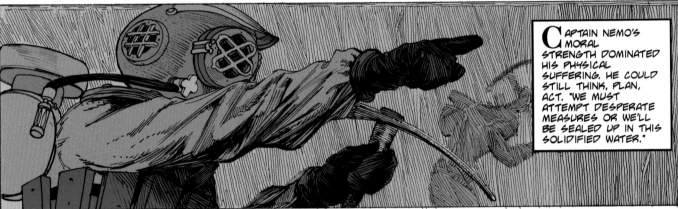

Captain NEMO'S MORAL STRENGTH DOMINATED HIS PHYSICAL SUFFERING. HE COULD STILL THINK, PLAN, ACT. "WE MUST ATTEMPT DESPERATE MEASURES OR WE'LL BE SEALED UP IN THIS SOLIDIFIED WATER."

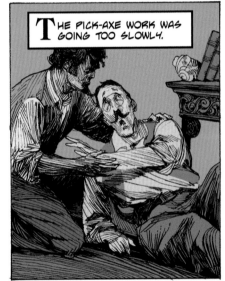

The PICK-AXE WORK WAS GOING TOO SLOWLY.

At THE CAPTAIN'S ORDERS, THE SHIP WAS RAISED OFF THE ICE AND MANEUVERED DIRECTLY ABOVE THE TRENCH WE HAD DUG.

CARRIED DOWN BY ITS TERRIFIC EXCESS WEIGHT, THE NAUTILUS SANK. THE REMAINING ICE BEGAN TO BREAK UP AS THE SHIP CONTINUED SINKING.

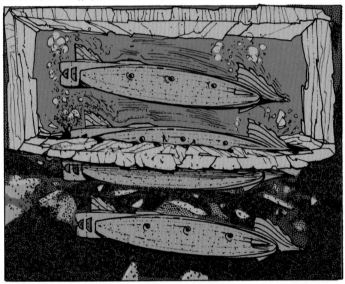

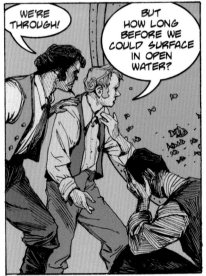

WE'RE THROUGH!

BUT HOW LONG BEFORE WE COULD SURFACE IN OPEN WATER?

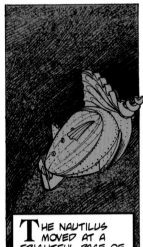

The NAUTILUS MOVED AT A FRIGHTFUL PACE OF FORTY KNOTS.

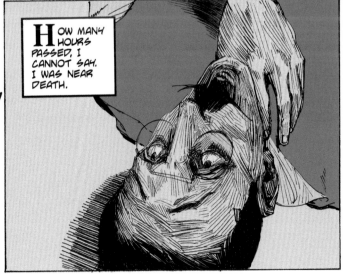

How MANY HOURS PASSED, I CANNOT SAY. I WAS NEAR DEATH.

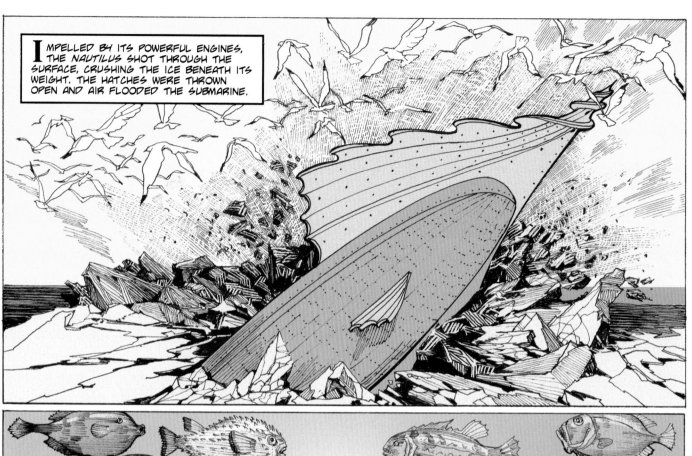

IMPELLED BY ITS POWERFUL ENGINES, THE *NAUTILUS* SHOT THROUGH THE SURFACE, CRUSHING THE ICE BENEATH ITS WEIGHT. THE HATCHES WERE THROWN OPEN AND AIR FLOODED THE SUBMARINE.

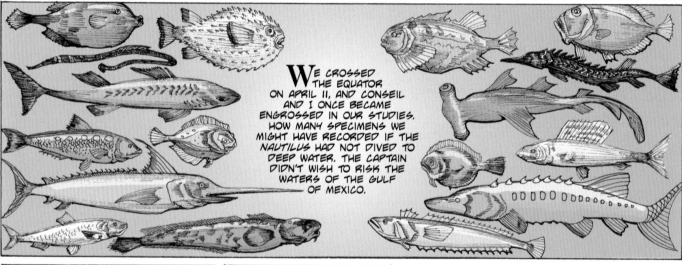

WE CROSSED THE EQUATOR ON APRIL 11, AND CONSEIL AND I ONCE BECAME ENGROSSED IN OUR STUDIES. HOW MANY SPECIMENS WE MIGHT HAVE RECORDED IF THE *NAUTILUS* HAD NOT DIVED TO DEEP WATER. THE CAPTAIN DIDN'T WISH TO RISK THE WATERS OF THE GULF OF MEXICO.

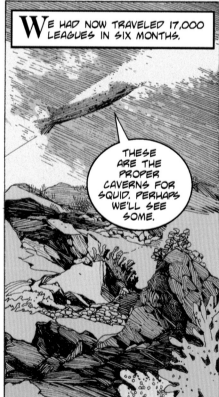

WE HAD NOW TRAVELED 17,000 LEAGUES IN SIX MONTHS.

THESE ARE THE PROPER CAVERNS FOR SQUID. PERHAPS WE'LL SEE SOME.

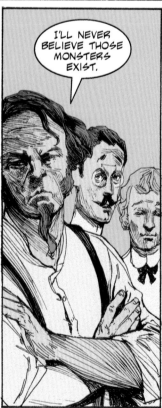

I'LL NEVER BELIEVE THOSE MONSTERS EXIST.

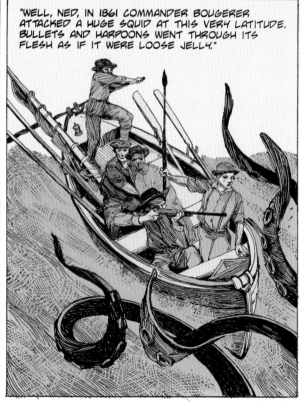

"WELL, NED, IN 1861 COMMANDER BOUGERER ATTACKED A HUGE SQUID AT THIS VERY LATITUDE. BULLETS AND HARPOONS WENT THROUGH ITS FLESH AS IF IT WERE LOOSE JELLY."

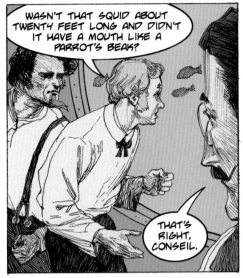

WASN'T THAT SQUID ABOUT TWENTY FEET LONG AND DIDN'T IT HAVE A MOUTH LIKE A PARROT'S BEAK?

THAT'S RIGHT, CONSEIL.

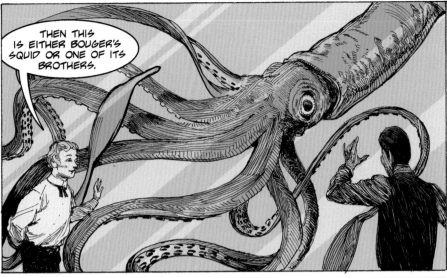

THEN THIS IS EITHER BOUGER'S SQUID OR ONE OF ITS BROTHERS.

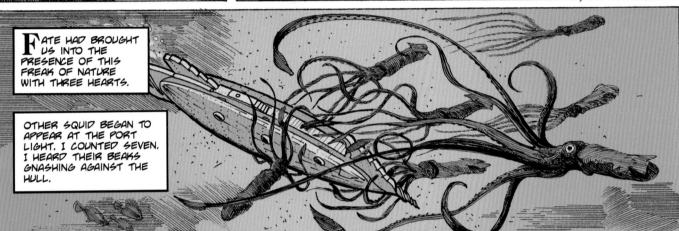

FATE HAD BROUGHT US INTO THE PRESENCE OF THIS FREAK OF NATURE WITH THREE HEARTS.

OTHER SQUID BEGAN TO APPEAR AT THE PORT LIGHT. I COUNTED SEVEN. I HEARD THEIR BEAKS GNASHING AGAINST THE HULL.

SUDDENLY, THE NAUTILUS TREMBLED AND STOPPED.

A CURIOUS COLLECTION OF POULPS.

YES, MR. NATURALIST--AND WE ARE GOING TO FIGHT THEM MAN TO BEAST. THE SCREW HAS STOPPED. A SQUID GOT ITS BEAK ENTANGLED IN OUR BLADES.

I'M GOING TO SURFACE AND SLAUGHTER THIS VERMIN.

THE HATCHES WERE OPENED. IMMEDIATELY, TENTACLES SLID DOWN THE STAIRCASE AND LIFTED AN UNFORTUNATE SAILOR OUT ONTO THE PLATFORM.

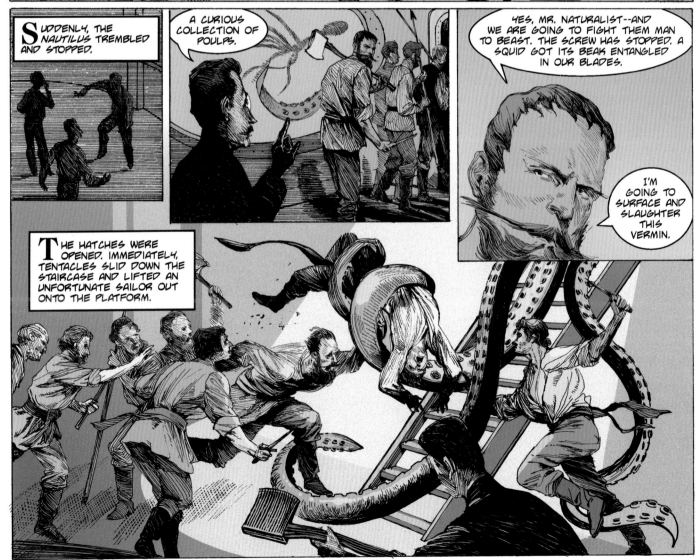

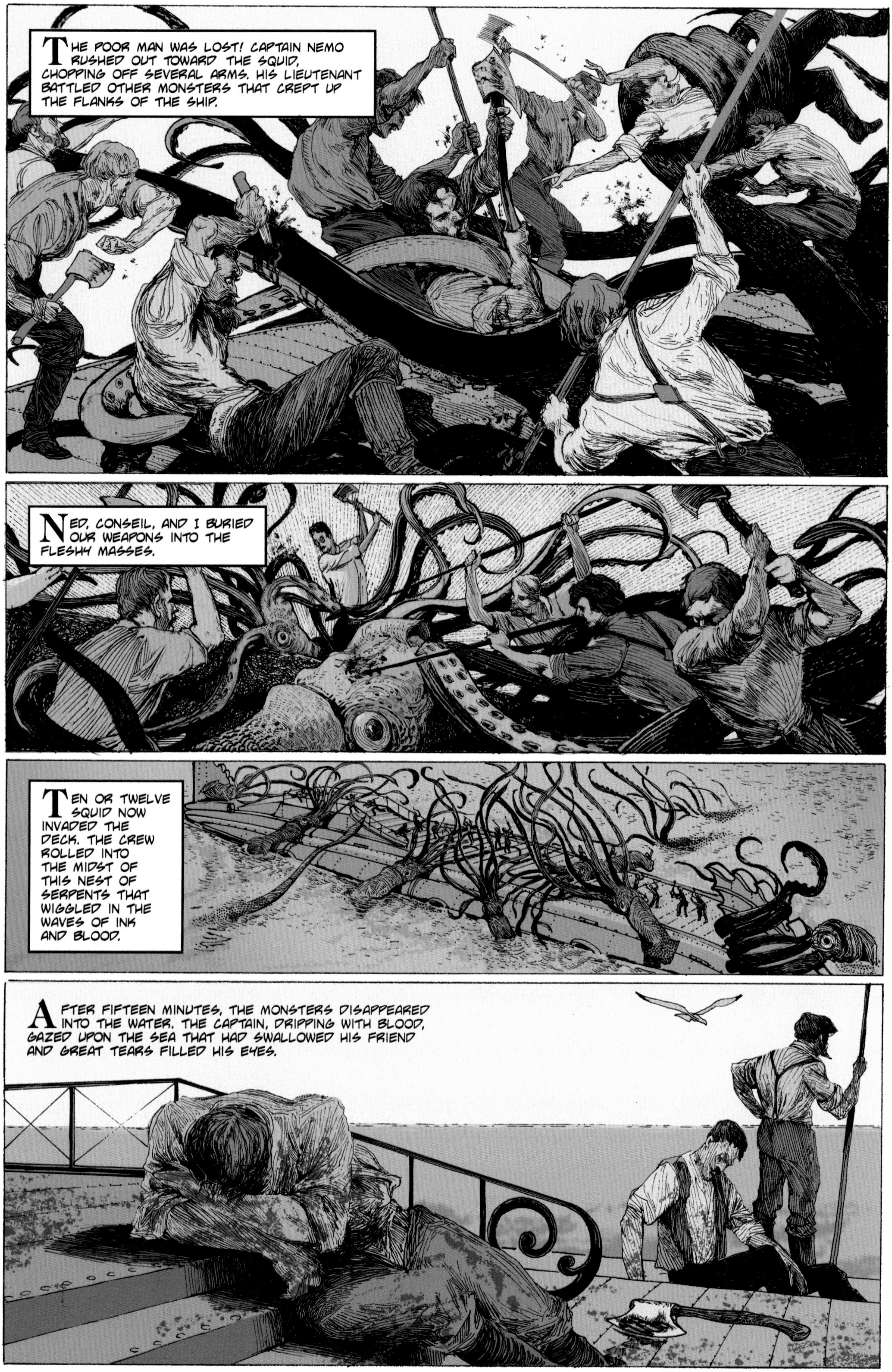
THE POOR MAN WAS LOST! CAPTAIN NEMO RUSHED OUT TOWARD THE SQUID, CHOPPING OFF SEVERAL ARMS. HIS LIEUTENANT BATTLED OTHER MONSTERS THAT CREPT UP THE FLANKS OF THE SHIP.
NED, CONSEIL, AND I BURIED OUR WEAPONS INTO THE FLESHY MASSES.
TEN OR TWELVE SQUID NOW INVADED THE DECK. THE CREW ROLLED INTO THE MIDST OF THIS NEST OF SERPENTS THAT WIGGLED IN THE WAVES OF INK AND BLOOD.
AFTER FIFTEEN MINUTES, THE MONSTERS DISAPPEARED INTO THE WATER. THE CAPTAIN, DRIPPING WITH BLOOD, GAZED UPON THE SEA THAT HAD SWALLOWED HIS FRIEND AND GREAT TEARS FILLED HIS EYES.

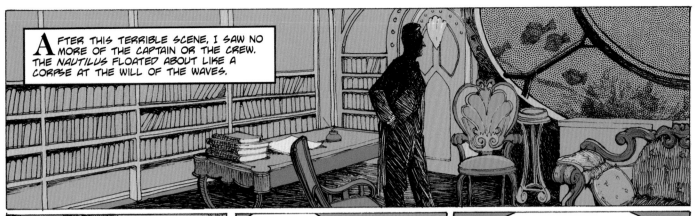

AFTER THIS TERRIBLE SCENE, I SAW NO MORE OF THE CAPTAIN OR THE CREW. THE *NAUTILUS* FLOATED ABOUT LIKE A CORPSE AT THE WILL OF THE WAVES.

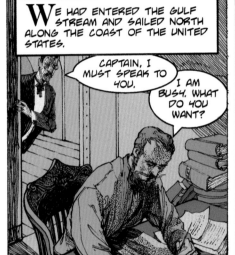

WE HAD ENTERED THE GULF STREAM AND SAILED NORTH ALONG THE COAST OF THE UNITED STATES.

CAPTAIN, I MUST SPEAK TO YOU.

I AM BUSY. WHAT DO YOU WANT?

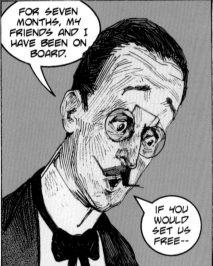

FOR SEVEN MONTHS, MY FRIENDS AND I HAVE BEEN ON BOARD.

IF YOU WOULD SET US FREE--

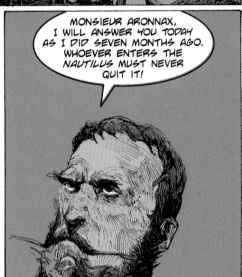

MONSIEUR ARONNAX, I WILL ANSWER YOU TODAY AS I DID SEVEN MONTHS AGO. WHOEVER ENTERS THE *NAUTILUS* MUST NEVER QUIT IT!

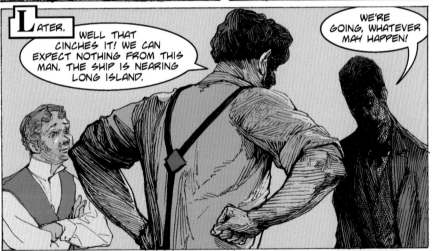

LATER.

WELL THAT CINCHES IT! WE CAN EXPECT NOTHING FROM THIS MAN. THE SHIP IS NEARING LONG ISLAND.

WE'RE GOING, WHATEVER MAY HAPPEN!

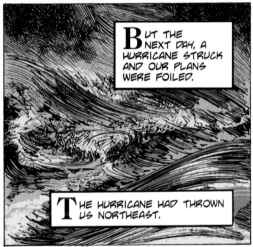

BUT THE NEXT DAY, A HURRICANE STRUCK AND OUR PLANS WERE FOILED.

THE HURRICANE HAD THROWN US NORTHEAST.

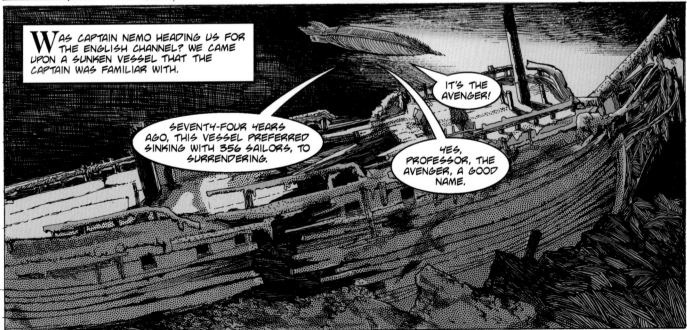

WAS CAPTAIN NEMO HEADING US FOR THE ENGLISH CHANNEL? WE CAME UPON A SUNKEN VESSEL THAT THE CAPTAIN WAS FAMILIAR WITH.

SEVENTY-FOUR YEARS AGO, THIS VESSEL PREFERRED SINKING WITH 356 SAILORS, TO SURRENDERING.

IT'S THE AVENGER!

YES, PROFESSOR, THE AVENGER, A GOOD NAME.

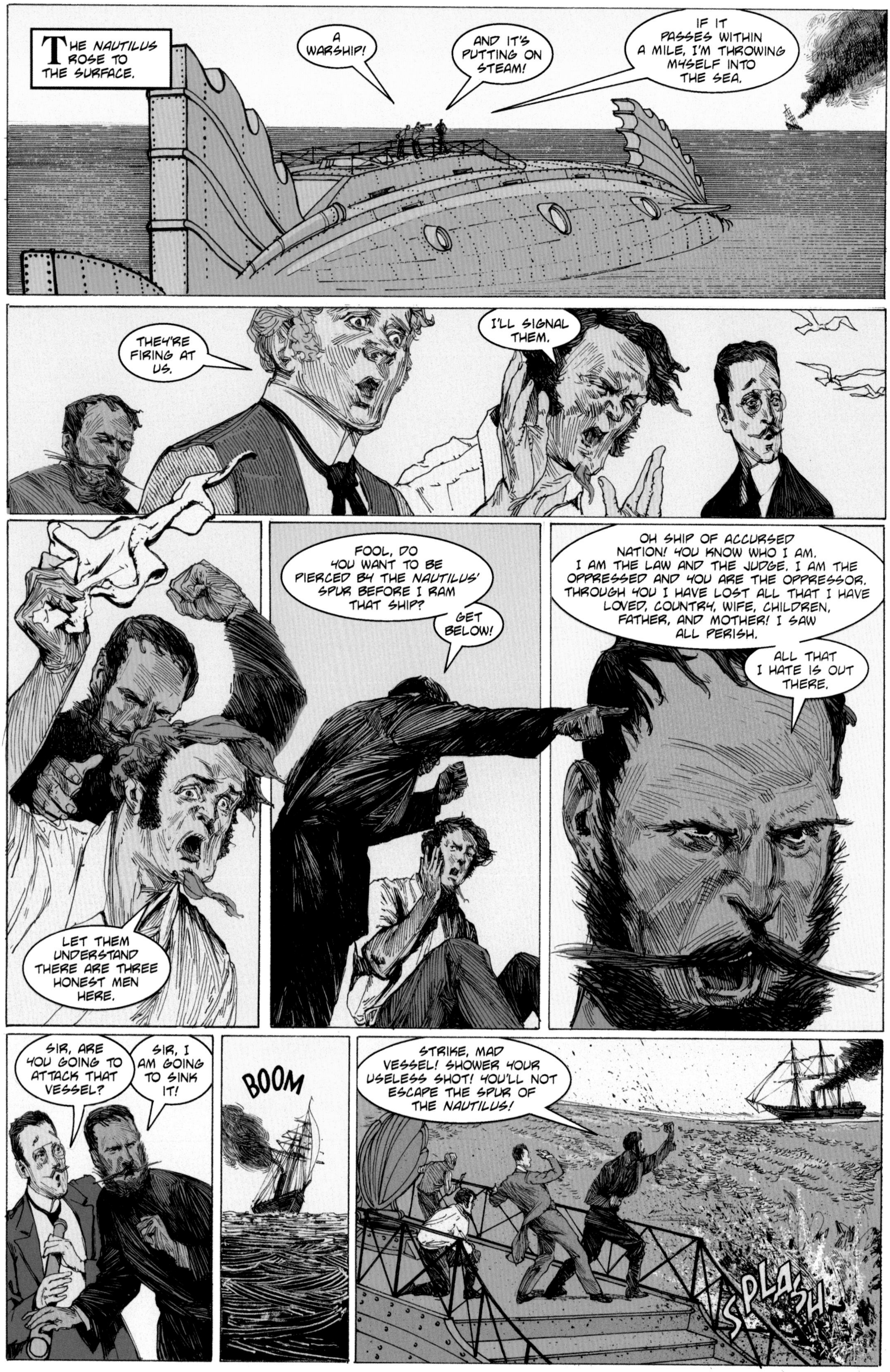
THE NAUTILUS ROSE TO THE SURFACE.
A WARSHIP!
AND IT'S PUTTING ON STEAM!
IF IT PASSES WITHIN A MILE, I'M THROWING MYSELF INTO THE SEA.
THEY'RE FIRING AT US.
I'LL SIGNAL THEM.
LET THEM UNDERSTAND THERE ARE THREE HONEST MEN HERE.
FOOL, DO YOU WANT TO BE PIERCED BY THE NAUTILUS' SPUR BEFORE I RAM THAT SHIP?
GET BELOW!
OH SHIP OF ACCURSED NATION! YOU KNOW WHO I AM. I AM THE LAW AND THE JUDGE. I AM THE OPPRESSED AND YOU ARE THE OPPRESSOR. THROUGH YOU I HAVE LOST ALL THAT I HAVE LOVED, COUNTRY, WIFE, CHILDREN, FATHER, AND MOTHER! I SAW ALL PERISH.
ALL THAT I HATE IS OUT THERE.
SIR, ARE YOU GOING TO ATTACK THAT VESSEL?
SIR, I AM GOING TO SINK IT!
BOOM
STRIKE, MAD VESSEL! SHOWER YOUR USELESS SHOT! YOU'LL NOT ESCAPE THE SPUR OF THE NAUTILUS!
SPLASH

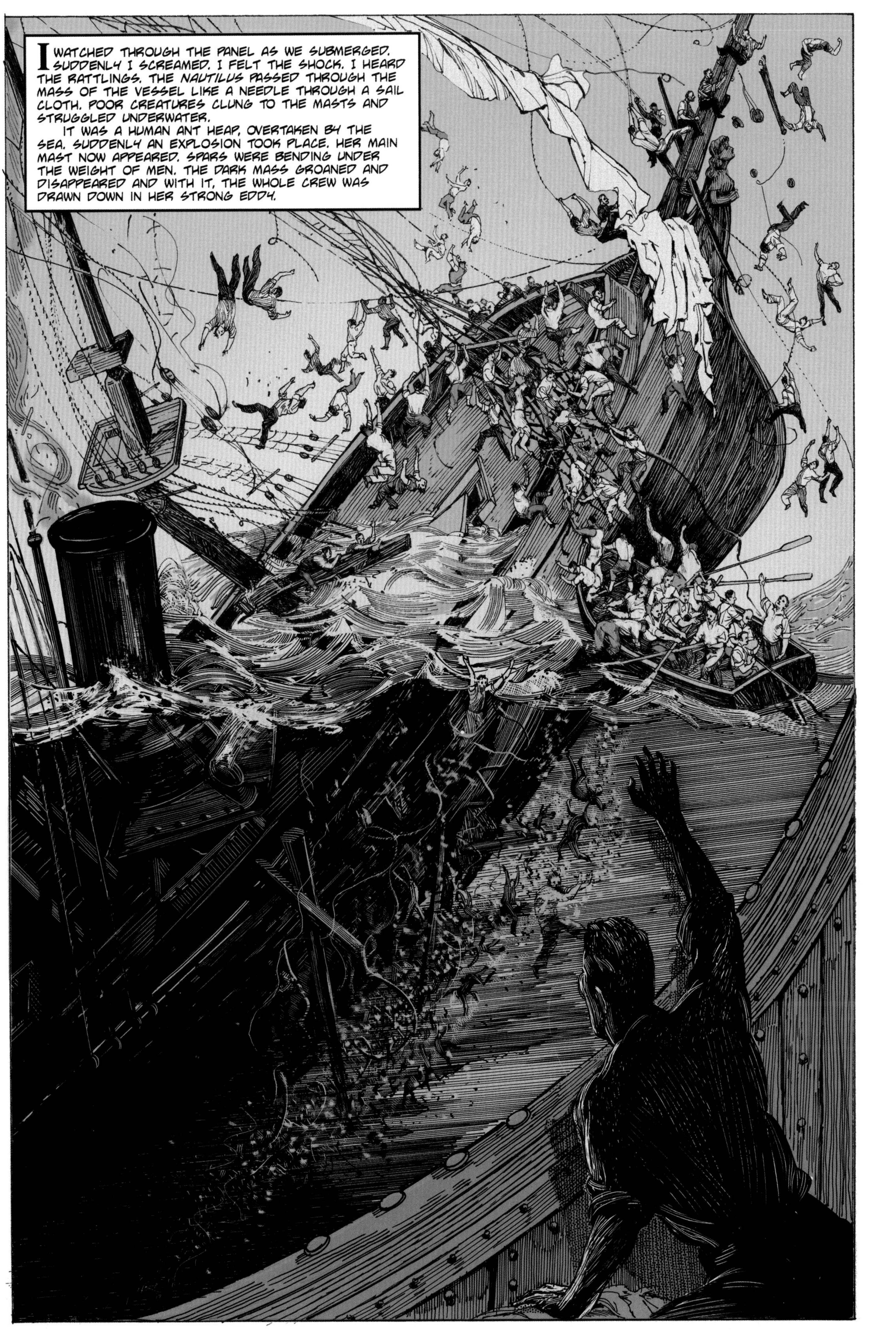
I WATCHED THROUGH THE PANEL AS WE SUBMERGED. SUDDENLY I SCREAMED. I FELT THE SHOCK. I HEARD THE RATTLINGS. THE *NAUTILUS* PASSED THROUGH THE MASS OF THE VESSEL LIKE A NEEDLE THROUGH A SAIL CLOTH. POOR CREATURES CLUNG TO THE MASTS AND STRUGGLED UNDERWATER.
IT WAS A HUMAN ANT HEAP, OVERTAKEN BY THE SEA. SUDDENLY AN EXPLOSION TOOK PLACE. HER MAIN MAST NOW APPEARED. SPARS WERE BENDING UNDER THE WEIGHT OF MEN. THE DARK MASS GROANED AND DISAPPEARED AND WITH IT, THE WHOLE CREW WAS DRAWN DOWN IN HER STRONG EDDY.

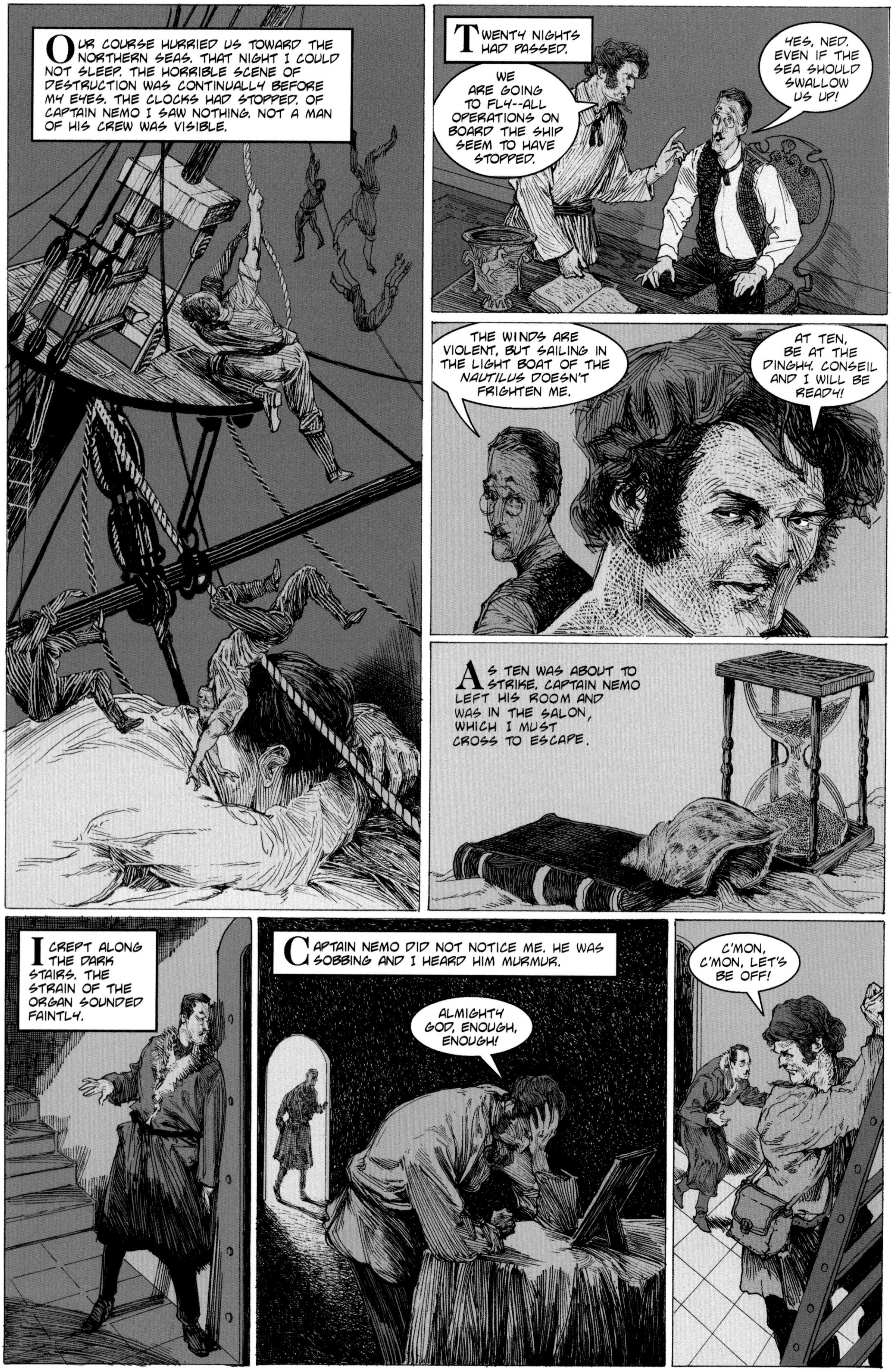
OUR COURSE HURRIED US TOWARD THE NORTHERN SEAS. THAT NIGHT I COULD NOT SLEEP. THE HORRIBLE SCENE OF DESTRUCTION WAS CONTINUALLY BEFORE MY EYES. THE CLOCKS HAD STOPPED. OF CAPTAIN NEMO I SAW NOTHING. NOT A MAN OF HIS CREW WAS VISIBLE.
TWENTY NIGHTS HAD PASSED.
WE ARE GOING TO FLY--ALL OPERATIONS ON BOARD THE SHIP SEEM TO HAVE STOPPED.
YES, NED, EVEN IF THE SEA SHOULD SWALLOW US UP!
THE WINDS ARE VIOLENT, BUT SAILING IN THE LIGHT BOAT OF THE NAUTILUS DOESN'T FRIGHTEN ME.
AT TEN, BE AT THE DINGHY. CONSEIL AND I WILL BE READY!
AS TEN WAS ABOUT TO STRIKE, CAPTAIN NEMO LEFT HIS ROOM AND WAS IN THE SALON, WHICH I MUST CROSS TO ESCAPE.
I CREPT ALONG THE DARK STAIRS. THE STRAIN OF THE ORGAN SOUNDED FAINTLY.
CAPTAIN NEMO DID NOT NOTICE ME. HE WAS SOBBING AND I HEARD HIM MURMUR.
ALMIGHTY GOD, ENOUGH, ENOUGH!
C'MON, C'MON, LET'S BE OFF!

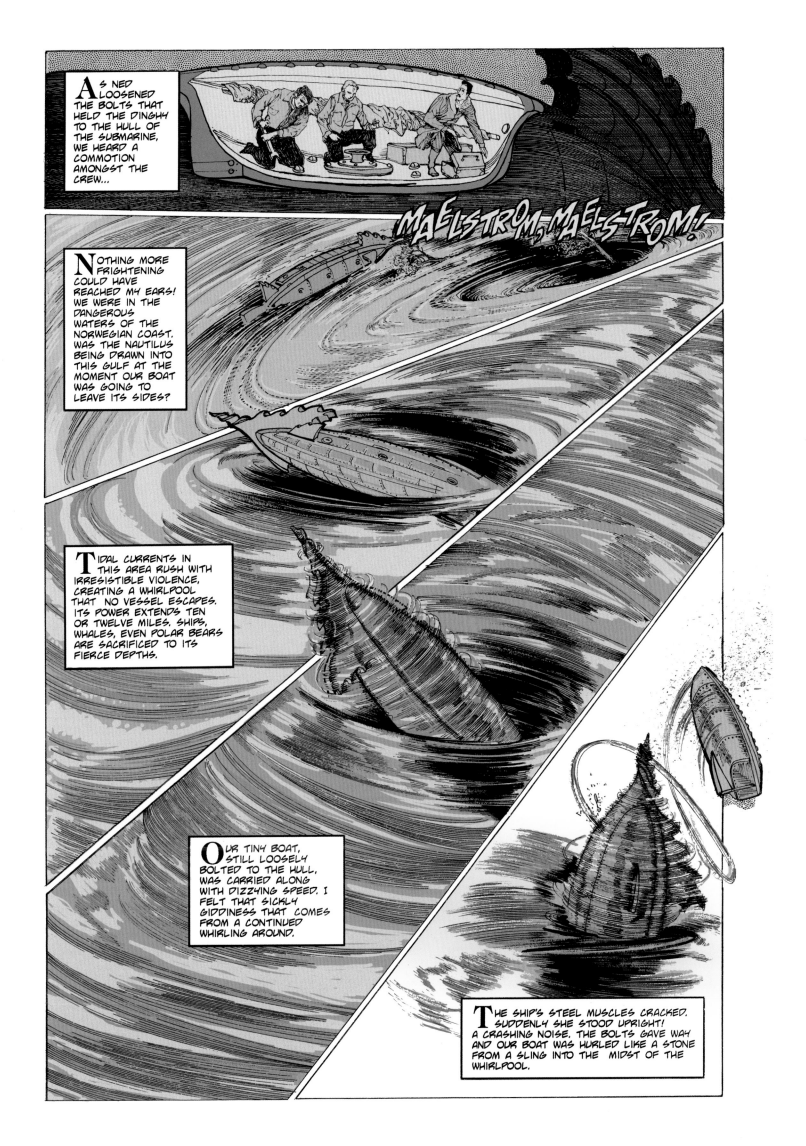

As Ned loosened the bolts that held the dinghy to the hull of the submarine, we heard a commotion amongst the crew...

MAELSTROM, MAELSTROM!

Nothing more frightening could have reached my ears! We were in the dangerous waters of the Norwegian coast. Was the Nautilus being drawn into this gulf at the moment our boat was going to leave its sides?

Tidal currents in this area rush with irresistible violence, creating a whirlpool that no vessel escapes. Its power extends ten or twelve miles. Ships, whales, even polar bears are sacrificed to its fierce depths.

Our tiny boat, still loosely bolted to the hull, was carried along with dizzying speed. I felt that sickly giddiness that comes from a continued whirling around.

The ship's steel muscles cracked. Suddenly she stood upright! A crashing noise. The bolts gave way and our boat was hurled like a stone from a sling into the midst of the whirlpool.

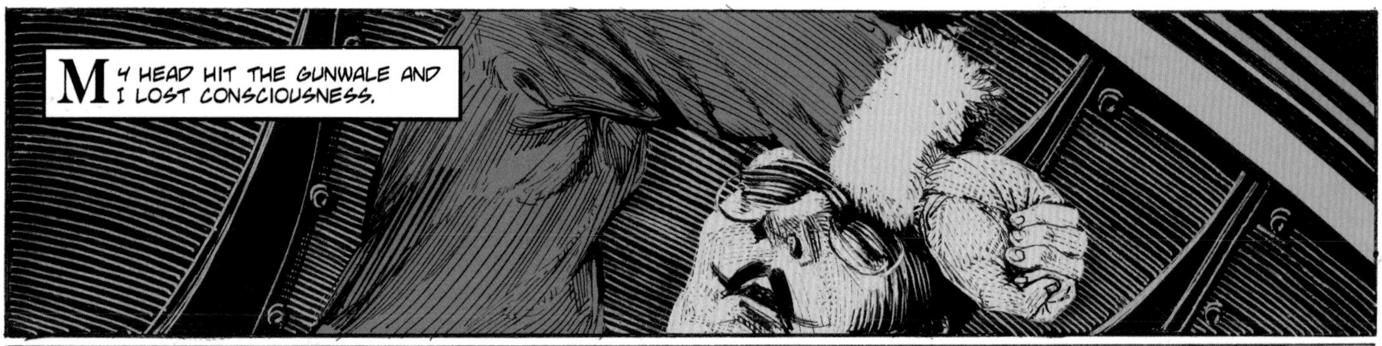
MY HEAD HIT THE GUNWALE AND I LOST CONSCIOUSNESS.

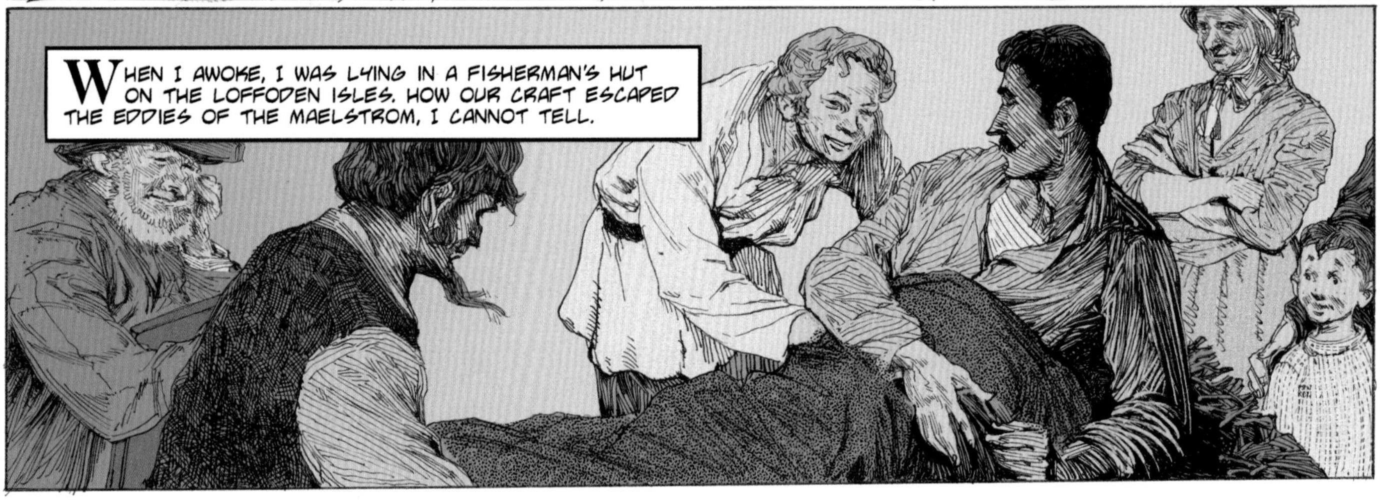
WHEN I AWOKE, I WAS LYING IN A FISHERMAN'S HUT ON THE LOFFODEN ISLES. HOW OUR CRAFT ESCAPED THE EDDIES OF THE MAELSTROM, I CANNOT TELL.

WHILE AMONG THESE WORTHY PEOPLE, I HAVE WRITTEN THIS NARRATIVE. WHAT ABOUT THE *NAUTILUS?* DID CAPTAIN NEMO RUN HIS SHIP INTO THE MAELSTROM VOLUNTARILY? DID HE SURVIVE? IF SO, MAY THE CAPTAIN'S SPIRIT OF VENGEANCE BE EXTINGUISHED. MAY THE JUDGE DISAPPEAR AND THE PHILOSOPHER CONTINUE HIS EXPLORATION.

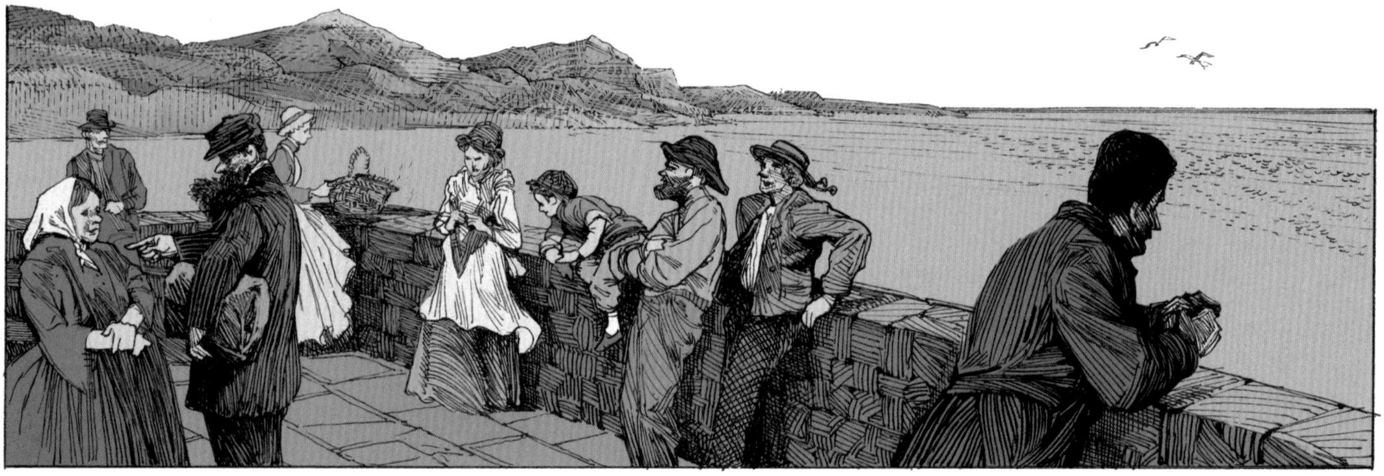

AND TO THE QUESTION ASKED BY ECCLESIASTES 3,000 YEARS AGO--

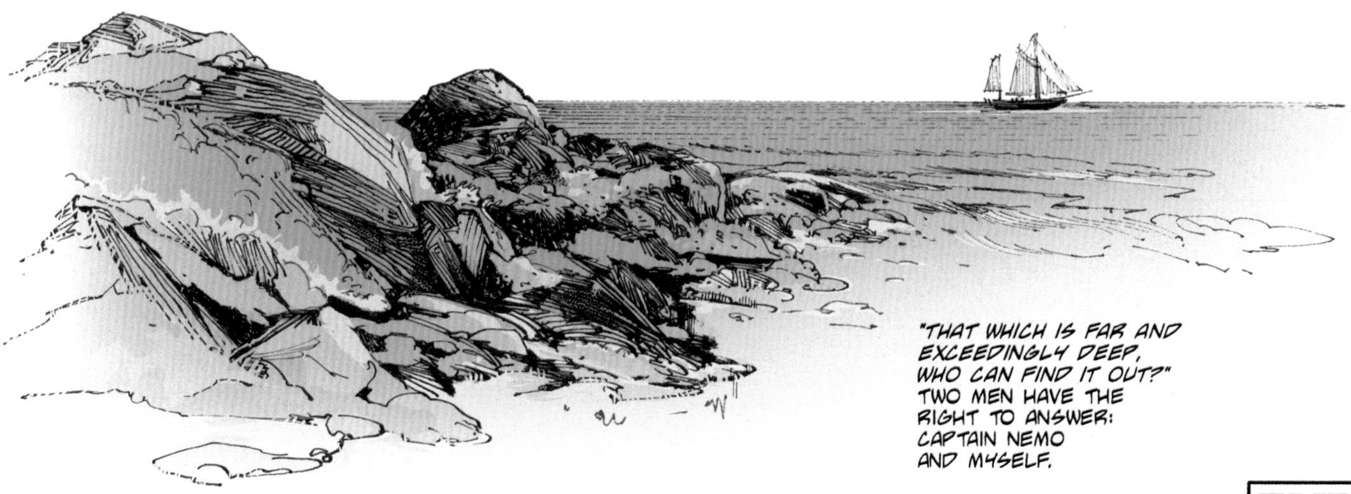
"THAT WHICH IS FAR AND EXCEEDINGLY DEEP, WHO CAN FIND IT OUT?" TWO MEN HAVE THE RIGHT TO ANSWER: CAPTAIN NEMO AND MYSELF.

END

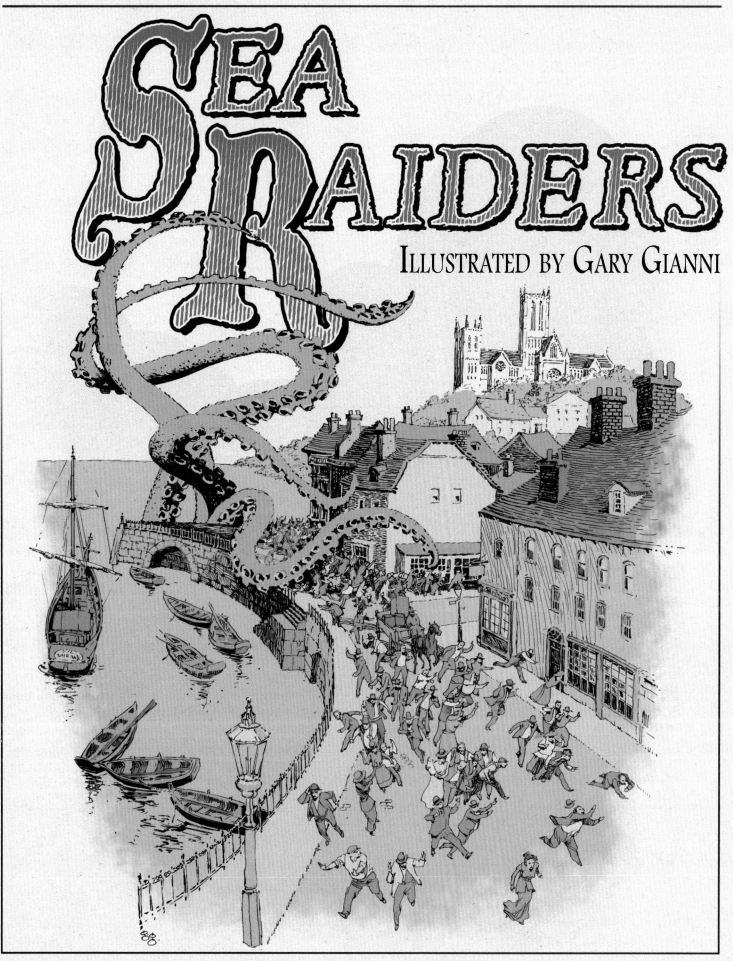

A THRILLING STORY OF THE DEEPS BY H. G. WELLS

SEA RAIDERS

ILLUSTRATED BY GARY GIANNI

CHAPTER I

Until the extraordinary affair at Sidmouth, the peculiar species *Haploteuthis ferox* was known to science only generically, on the strength of a half-digested tentacle obtained near the Azores, and a decaying body pecked by birds and nibbled by fish, found early in 1896 by Mr. Jennings, near Land's End.

In no department of zoological science, indeed, are we quite so much in the dark as with regard to the deep-sea cephalopods. A mere accident, for instance, it was that led to the Prince of Monaco's discovery of nearly a dozen new forms in the summer of 1895, a discovery in which the before-mentioned tentacle was included. It chanced that a cachalot was killed off Terceira by some sperm whalers, and in its last struggles charged almost to the Prince's yacht, missed it, rolled under, and died within twenty yards of his rudder. And in its agony it threw up a number of large objects, which the Prince, dimly perceiving they were strange and important, was, by a happy expedient, able to secure before they sank. He set his screws in motion, and kept them circling in the vortices thus created until a boat could be lowered. And these specimens were whole cephalopods and fragments of cephalopods, some of gigantic proportions, and almost all of them unknown to science!

It would seem, indeed, that these large and agile creatures, living in the middle depths of the sea, must, to a large extent, for ever remain unknown to us, since under water they are too nimble for nets, and it is only by such rare, unlooked-for accidents that specimens can be obtained. In the case of *Haploteuthis ferox*, for instance, we are still altogether ignorant of its habitat, as ignorant as we are of the breeding-ground of the herring or the sea-ways of the salmon. And zoologists are altogether at a loss to account for its sudden appearance on our coast. Possibly it was the stress of a hunger migration that drove it hither out of the deep. But it will be, perhaps, better to avoid necessarily inconclusive discussion, and to proceed at once with our narrative.

The first human being to set eyes upon a living *Haploteuthis*—the first human being to survive, that is, for there can be little doubt now that the wave of bathing fatalities and boating accidents that travelled along the coast of Cornwall and Devon in early May was due to this cause—was a retired tea-dealer of the name of Fison, who was stopping at a Sidmouth boarding-house. It was in the afternoon, and he was walking along the cliff path between Sidmouth and Ladram Bay. The cliffs in this direction are very high, but down the red face of them in one place a kind of ladder staircase has been made. He was near this when his attention was attracted by what at first he thought to be a cluster of birds struggling over a fragment of food that caught the sunlight, and glistened pinkish-white. The tide was right out, and this object was not only far below him, but remote across a broad waste of rock reefs covered with dark seaweed and interspersed with silvery shining tidal pools. And he was, moreover, dazzled by the brightness of the further water.

In a minute, regarding this again, he perceived that his judgment was in fault, for over this struggle circled a number of birds, jackdaws and gulls for the most part, the latter gleaming blindingly when the sunlight smote their wings, and they seemed minute in comparison with it. And his curiosity was, perhaps, aroused all the more strongly because of his first insufficient explanations.

As he had nothing better to do than amuse himself, he decided to make this object, whatever it was, the goal of his afternoon walk, instead of Ladram Bay, conceiving it might perhaps be a great fish of some sort, stranded by some chance, and flapping about in its distress. And so he hurried down the long steep ladder, stopping at intervals of thirty feet or so to take breath and scan the mysterious movement.

At the foot of the cliff he was, of course, nearer his object than he had been; but, on the other hand, it now came up against the incandescent sky, beneath the sun, so as to seem dark and indistinct. Whatever was pinkish of it was now hidden by a skerry of weedy boulders. But he perceived that it was made up of seven rounded bodies distinct or connected, and that the birds kept up a constant croaking and screaming, but seemed afraid to approach it too closely.

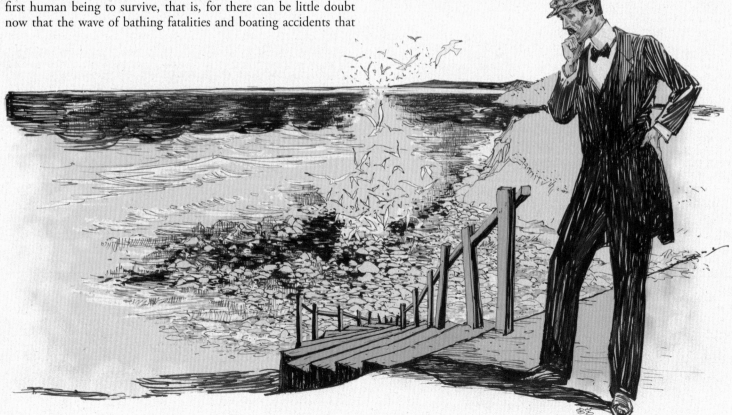

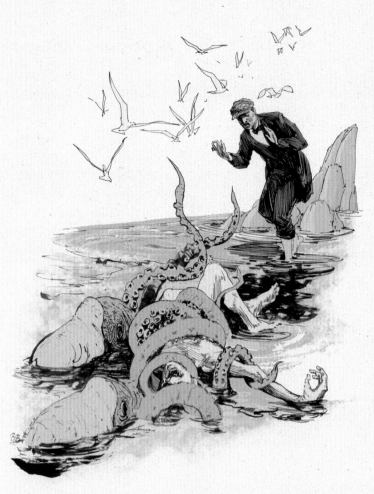

evil interest; but it does not appear that Mr. Fison was afraid, or that he realized that he was in any danger. Possibly his confidence is to be ascribed to the limpness of their attitudes. But he was horrified, of course, and intensely excited and indignant, at such revolting creatures preying upon human flesh. He thought they had chanced upon a drowned body. He shouted to them, with the idea of driving them off, and finding they did not budge, cast about him, picked up a big rounded lump of rock, and flung it at one.

And then, slowly uncoiling their tentacles, they all began moving towards him—creeping at first deliberately, and making a soft purring sound to each other.

In a moment Mr. Fison realized that he was in danger. He shouted again, threw both his boots, and started off, with a leap, forthwith. Twenty yards off he stopped and faced about, judging them slow, and behold! The tentacles of their leader were already pouring over the rocky ridge on which he had just been standing!

At that he shouted again, but this time not threatening, but a cry of dismay, and began jumping, striding, slipping, wading across the uneven expanse between him and the beach. The tall red cliffs seemed suddenly at a vast distance, and he saw, as though they were creatures in another world, two minute workmen engaged in the repair of the ladder-way, and little suspecting the race for life that was beginning below them. At one time he could hear the creatures splashing in the pools not a dozen feet behind him, and once he slipped and almost fell.

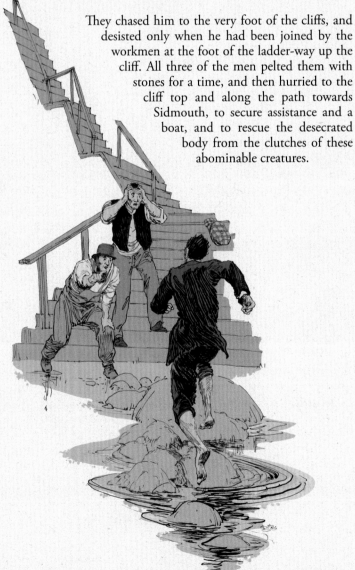

They chased him to the very foot of the cliffs, and desisted only when he had been joined by the workmen at the foot of the ladder-way up the cliff. All three of the men pelted them with stones for a time, and then hurried to the cliff top and along the path towards Sidmouth, to secure assistance and a boat, and to rescue the desecrated body from the clutches of these abominable creatures.

Mr. Fison, torn by curiosity, began picking his way across the wave-worn rocks, and finding the wet seaweed that covered them thickly rendered them extremely slippery, he stopped, removed his shoes and socks, and rolled his trousers above his knees. His object was, of course, merely to avoid stumbling into the rocky pools about him, and perhaps he was rather glad, as all men are, of an excuse to resume, even for a moment, the sensations of his boyhood. At any rate, it is to this, no doubt, that he owes his life.

He approached his mark with all the assurance which the absolute security of this country against all forms of animal life gives its inhabitants. The round bodies moved to and fro, but it was only when he surmounted the skerry of boulders I have mentioned that he realized the horrible nature of the discovery. It came upon him with some suddenness.

The rounded bodies fell apart as he came into sight over the ridge, and displayed the pinkish object to be the partially devoured body of a human being, but whether of a man or woman he was unable to say. And the rounded bodies were new and ghastly-looking creatures, in shape somewhat resembling an octopus, with huge and very long and flexible tentacles, coiled copiously on the ground. The skin had a glistening texture, unpleasant to see, like shiny leather. The downward bend of the tentacle-surrounded mouth, the curious excrescence at the bend, the tentacles, and the large intelligent eyes, gave the creatures a grotesque suggestion of a face. They were the size of a fair-sized swine about the body, and the tentacles seemed to him to be many feet in length. There were, he thinks, seven or eight at least of the creatures. Twenty yards beyond them, amid the surf of the now returning tide, two others were emerging from the sea. Their bodies lay flatly on the rocks, and their eyes regarded him with

CHAPTER II

And, as if he had not already been in sufficient peril that day, Mr. Fison went with the boat to point out the exact spot of his adventure.

As the tide was down, it required a considerable detour to reach the spot, and when at last they came off the ladder-way, the mangled body had disappeared. The water was now running in, submerging first one slab of slimy rock and then another, and the four men in the boat—the workmen, that is, the boatman, and Mr. Fison—now turned their attention from the bearings off shore to the water beneath the keel.

At first they could see little below them, save a dark jungle of laminaria, with an occasional darting fish. Their minds were set on adventure, and they expressed their disappointment freely. But presently they saw one of the monsters swimming through the water seaward, with a curious rolling motion that suggested to Mr. Fison the spinning roll of a captive balloon. Almost immediately after, the waving streamers of laminaria were extraordinarily perturbed, parted for a moment, and three of these beasts became darkly visible, struggling for what was probably some fragment of the drowned man. In a moment the copious olive-green ribbons had poured again over this writhing group.

At that all four men, greatly excited, began beating the water with oars and shouting, and immediately they saw a tumultuous movement among the weeds. They desisted to see more clearly, and as soon as the water was smooth, they saw, as it seemed to them, the whole sea bottom among the weeds set with eyes.

"Ugly swine!" cried one of the men. "Why, there's dozens!"

And forthwith the things began to rise through the water about them.

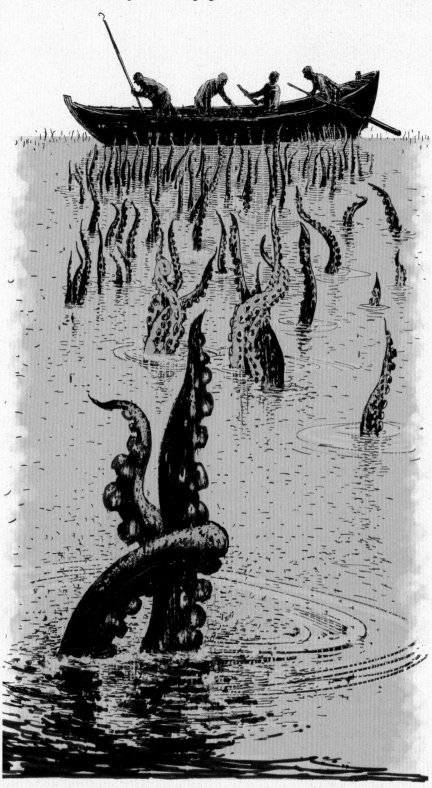

Mr. Fison has since described to the writer this startling eruption out of the waving laminaria meadows. To him it seemed to occupy a considerable time, but it is probable that really it was an affair of a few seconds only. For a time nothing but eyes, and then he speaks of tentacles streaming out and parting the weed fronds this way and that. Then these things, growing larger, until at last the bottom was hidden by their intercoiling forms, and the tips of tentacles rose darkly here and there into the air above the swell of the waters.

One came up boldly to the side of the boat, and clinging to this with three of its sucker-set tentacles, threw four others over the gunwale, as if with an intention either of oversetting the boat or of clambering into it. Mr. Fison at once caught up the boat-hook, and, jabbing furiously at the soft tentacles, forced it to desist. He was struck in the back and almost pitched overboard by the boatman, who was using his oar to resist a similar attack on the other side of the boat. But the tentacles on either side at once relaxed their hold, slid out of sight, and splashed into the water.

"We'd better get out of this," said Mr. Fison, who was trembling violently. He went to the tiller, while the boatman and one of the workmen seated themselves and began rowing. The other workman stood up in the fore part of the boat, with the boat-hook, ready to strike any more tentacles that might appear. Nothing else seems to have been said. Mr. Fison had expressed the common feeling beyond amendment. In a hushed, scared mood, with faces white and drawn, they set about escaping from the position into which they had so recklessly blundered.

But the oars had scarcely dropped into the water before dark, tapering, serpentine ropes had bound them, and were about the rudder; and creeping up the sides of the boat with a looping motion came the suckers again. The men gripped their oars and pulled, but it was like trying to move a boat in a floating raft of weeds. "Help here!" cried the boatman, and Mr. Fison and the second workman rushed to help lug at the oar.

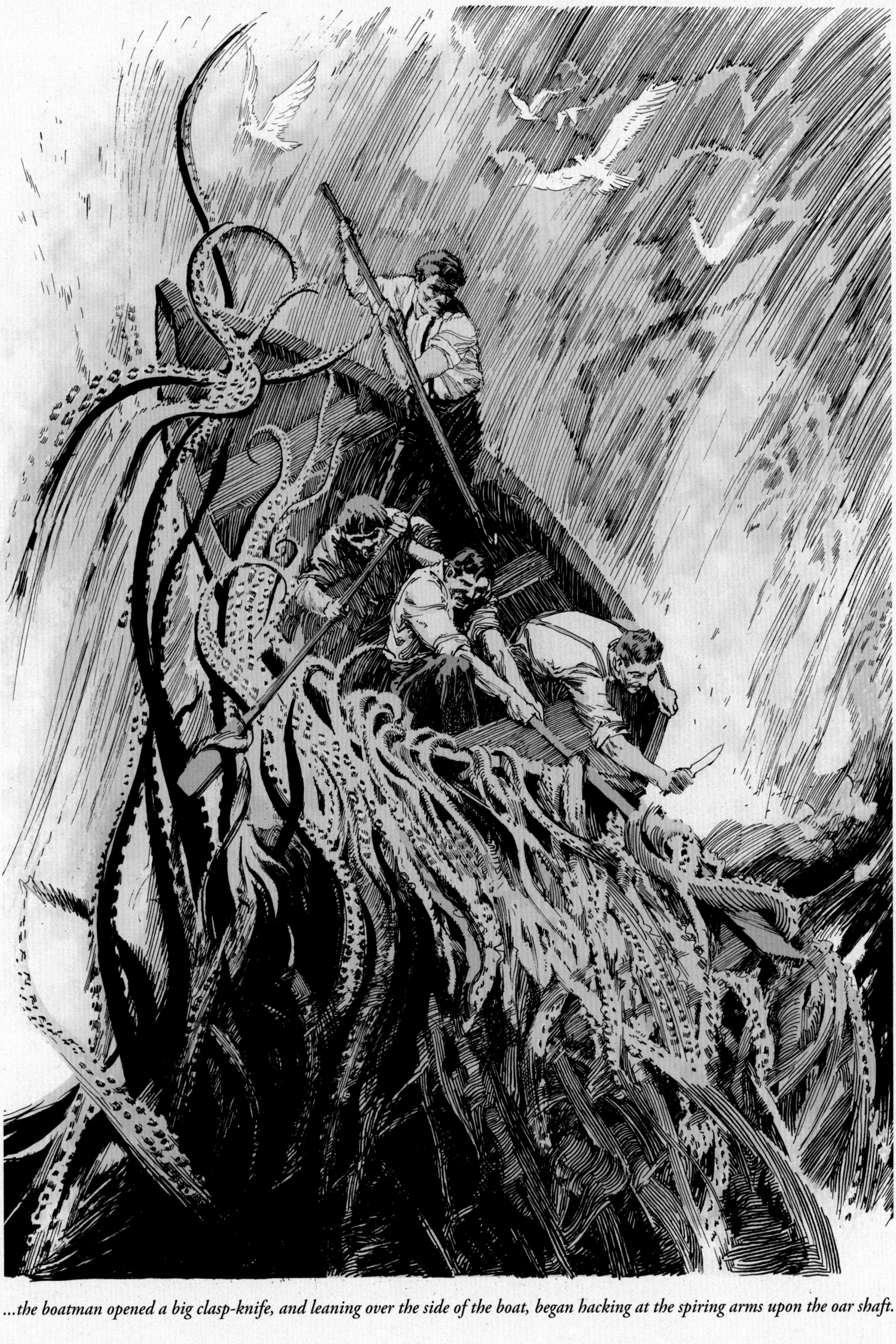

...the boatman opened a big clasp-knife, and leaning over the side of the boat, began hacking at the spiring arms upon the oar shaft.

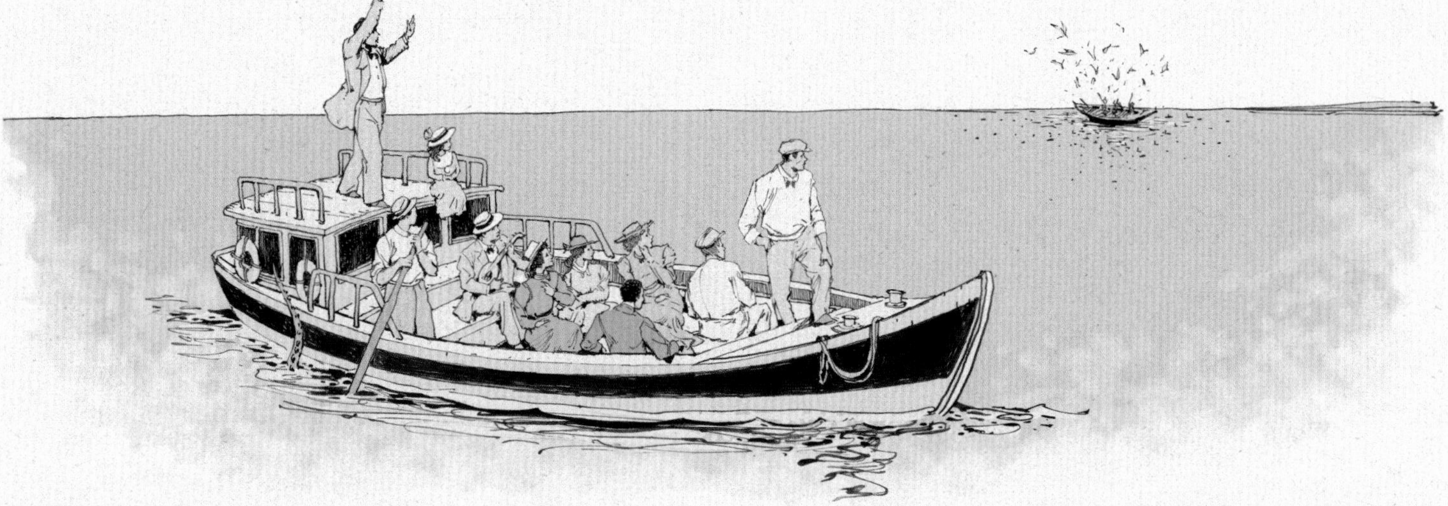

Then the man with the boat-hook—his name was Ewan, or Ewen—sprang up with a curse and began striking downward over the side, as far as he could reach, at the bank of tentacles that now clustered along the boat's bottom. And, at the same time, the two rowers stood up to get a better purchase for the recovery of their oars. The boatman handed his to Mr. Fison, who lugged desperately, and, meanwhile, the boatman opened a big clasp-knife, and leaning over the side of the boat, began hacking at the spiring arms upon the oar shaft.

Mr. Fison, staggering with the quivering rocking of the boat, his teeth set, his breath coming short, and the veins starting on his hands as he pulled at his oar, suddenly cast his eyes seaward. And there, not fifty yards off, across the long rollers of the incoming tide, was a large boat standing in towards them, with three women and a little child in it. A boatman was rowing, and a little man in a pink-ribboned straw hat and whites stood in the stern hailing them. For a moment, of course, Mr. Fison thought of help, and then he thought of the child. He abandoned his oar forthwith, threw up his arms in a frantic gesture, and screamed to the party in the boat to keep away "for God's sake!" It says much for the modesty and courage of Mr. Fison that he does not seem to be aware that there was any quality of heroism in his action at this juncture. The oar he had abandoned was at once drawn under, and presently reappeared floating about twenty yards away.

At the same moment Mr. Fison felt the boat under him lurch violently, and a hoarse scream, a prolonged cry of terror from Hill, the boatman, caused him to forget the party of excursionists altogether. He turned, and saw Hill crouching by the forward row-lock, his face convulsed with terror, and his right arm over the side and drawn tightly down. He gave now a succession of short, sharp cries, "Oh! oh! oh!—oh!" Mr. Fison believes that he must have been hacking at the tentacles below the water-line, and have been grasped by them, but, of course, it is quite impossible to say now certainly what had happened. The boat was heeling over, so that the gunwale was within ten inches of the water, and both Ewan and the other labourer were striking down into the water, with oar and boathook, on either side of Hill's arm. Mr. Fison instinctively placed himself to counterpoise them.

Then Hill, who was a burly, powerful man, made a strenuous effort, and rose almost to a standing position.

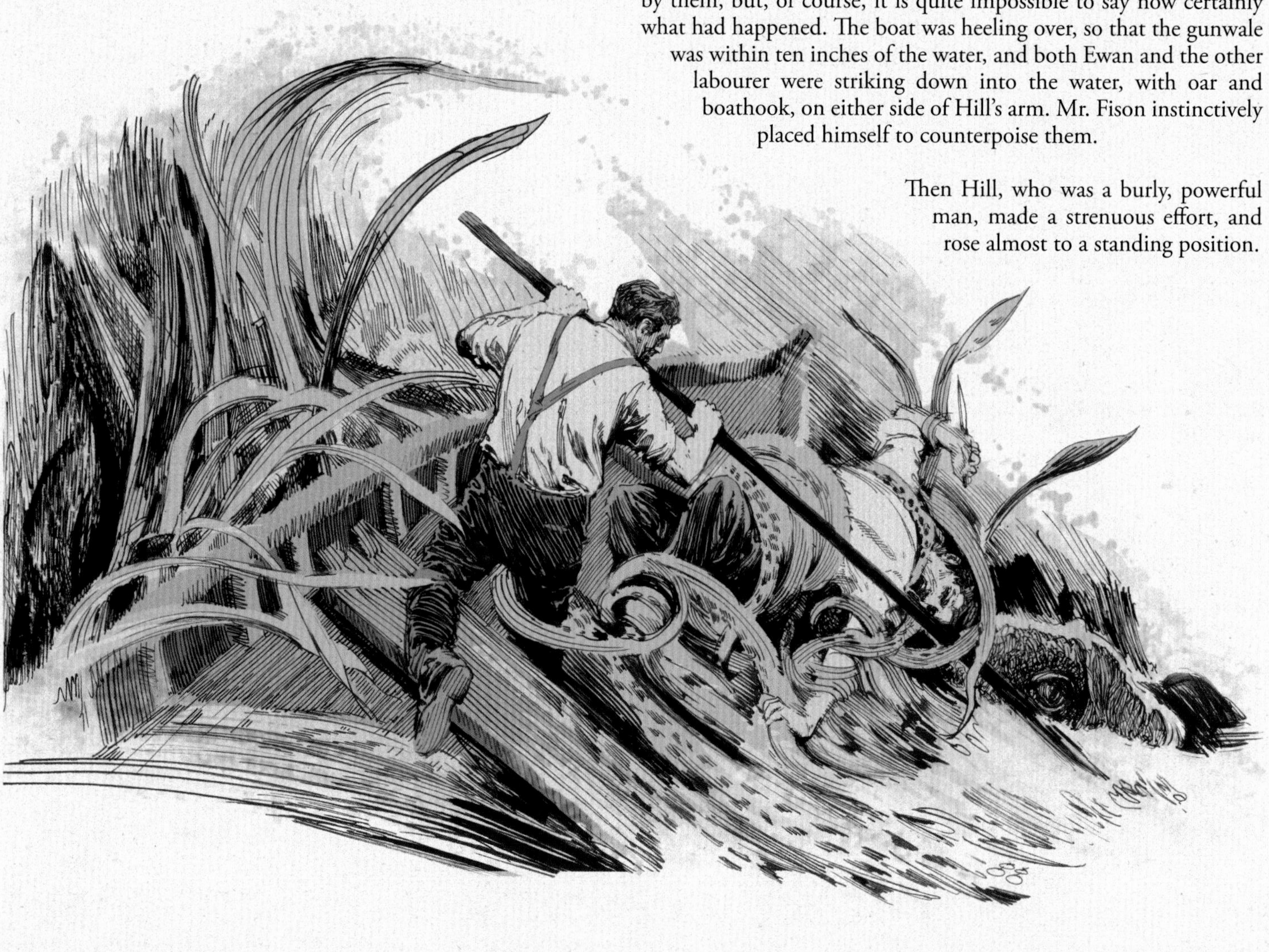

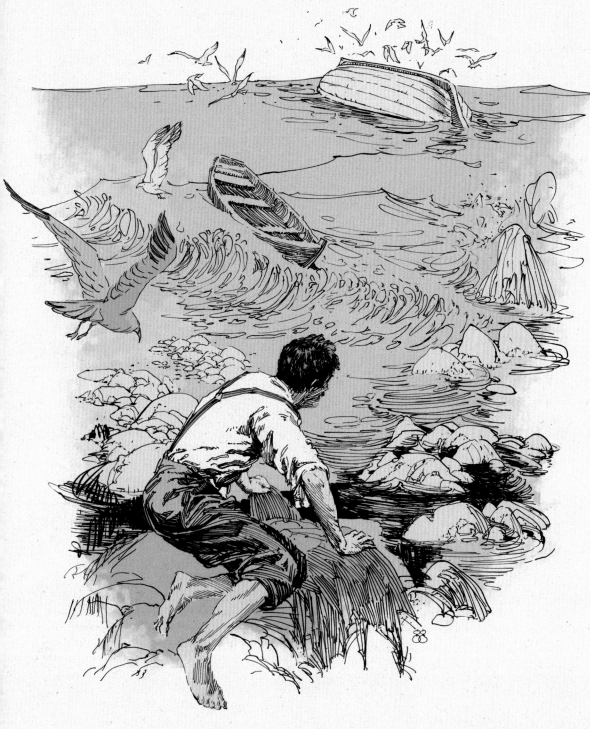

off a table of rock still rose in rhythmic movements above the inwash of the tide. In a moment Mr. Fison seized the oar from Ewan, gave one vigorous stroke, then dropping it, ran to the bows and leapt. He felt his feet slide over the rock, and, by a frantic effort, leapt again towards a further mass. He stumbled over this, came to his knees, and rose again.

"Look out!" cried someone, and a large drab body struck him. He was knocked flat into a tidal pool by one of the workmen, and as he went down he heard smothered, choking cries, that he believed at the time came from Hill. Then he found himself marvelling at the shrillness and variety of Hill's voice. Someone jumped over him, and a curving rush of foamy water poured over him, and passed. He scrambled to his feet dripping, and without looking seaward, ran as fast as his terror would let him shoreward. Before him, over the flat space of scattered rocks, stumbled the two workmen—one a dozen yards in front of the other.

He looked over his shoulder at last, and seeing that he was not pursued, faced about. He was astonished. From the moment of the rising of the cephalopods out of the water he had been acting too swiftly to fully comprehend his actions. Now it seemed to him as if he had suddenly jumped out of an evil dream.

For there were the sky, cloudless and blazing with the afternoon sun, the sea weltering under its pitiless brightness, the soft creamy foam of the breaking water, and the low, long, dark ridges of rock. The righted boat floated, rising and falling gently on the swell about a dozen yards from shore. Hill and the monsters, all the stress and tumult of that fierce fight for life, had vanished as though they had never been.

Mr. Fison's heart was beating violently; he was throbbing to the finger-tips, and his breath came deep.

There was something missing. For some seconds he could not think clearly enough what this might be. Sun, sky, sea, rocks—what was it? Then he remembered the boat-load of excursionists. It had vanished. He wondered whether he had imagined it. He turned, and saw the

He lifted his arm, indeed, clean out of the water. Hanging to it was a complicated tangle of brown ropes, and the eyes of one of the brutes that had hold of him, glaring straight and resolute, showed momentarily above the surface. The boat heeled more and more, and the green-brown water came pouring in a cascade over the side. Then Hill slipped and fell with his ribs across the side, and his arm and the mass of tentacles about it splashed back into the water. He rolled over; his boot kicked Mr. Fison's knee as that gentleman rushed forward to seize him, and in another moment fresh tentacles had whipped about his waist and neck, and after a brief, convulsive struggle, in which the boat was nearly capsized, Hill was lugged overboard. The boat righted with a violent jerk that all but sent Mr. Fison over the other side, and hid the struggle in the water from his eyes.

He stood staggering to recover his balance for a moment, and as he did so he became aware that the struggle and the inflowing tide had carried them close upon the weedy rocks again. Not four yards two workmen standing side by side under the projecting masses of the tall pink cliffs. He hesitated whether he should make one last attempt to save the man Hill. His physical excitement seemed to desert him suddenly, and leave him aimless and helpless. He turned shoreward, stumbling and wading towards his two companions.

He looked back again, and there were now two boats floating, and the one farthest out at sea pitched clumsily, bottom upward.

CHAPTER III

So it was *Haploteuthis ferox* made its appearance upon the Devonshire coast. So far, this has been its most serious aggression. Mr. Fison's account, taken together with the wave of boating and bathing casualties to which I have already alluded, and the absence of fish from the Cornish coasts that year, points clearly to a shoal of these voracious deep-sea monsters prowling slowly along the sub-tidal coast-line. Hunger migration has, I know, been suggested as the force that drove them hither; but, for my own part, I prefer to believe the alternative theory of Hemsley. Hemsley holds that a pack or shoal of these creatures may have become enamoured of human flesh by the accident of a foundered ship sinking among them, and have wandered in search of it out of their accustomed zone; first waylaying and following ships, and so coming to our shores in the wake of the Atlantic traffic. But to discuss Hemsley's cogent and admirably-stated arguments would be out of place here.

It would seem that the appetites of the shoal were satisfied by the catch of eleven people—for, so far as can be ascertained, there were ten people in the second boat, and certainly these creatures gave no further signs of their presence off Sidmouth that day. The coast between Seaton and Budleigh Salterton was patrolled all that evening and night by four Preventive Service boats, the men in which were armed with harpoons and cutlasses, and as the evening advanced, a number of more or less similarly equipped expeditions, organized by private individuals, joined them. Mr. Fison took no part in any of these expeditions.

About midnight excited hails were heard from a boat about a couple of miles out at sea to the south-east of Sidmouth, and a lantern was seen waving in a strange manner to and fro and up and down. The nearer boats at once hurried towards the alarm. The venturesome occupants of the boat—a seaman, a curate, and two schoolboys—had actually seen the monsters passing under their boat. The creatures, it seems, like most deep-sea organisms, were phosphorescent, and they had been floating, five fathoms deep or so, like creatures of moonshine through the blackness of the water, their tentacles retracted and as if asleep, rolling over and over, and moving slowly in a wedge-like formation towards the south-east.

These people told their story in gesticulated fragments, as first one boat drew alongside and then another. At last there was a little fleet of eight or nine boats collected together, and from them a tumult, like the chatter of a market-place, rose into the stillness of the night. These was little or no disposition to pursue the shoal, the people had neither weapons nor experience for such a dubious chase, and presently—even with a certain relief, it may be—the boats turned shoreward.

And now to tell what is perhaps the most astonishing fact in this whole astonishing raid. We have not the slightest knowledge of the subsequent movements of the shoal, although the whole south-west coast was now alert for it. But it may, perhaps, be significant that a cachalot was stranded off Sark on June 3. Two weeks and three days after this Sidmouth affair, a living *Haploteuthis* came ashore on Calais sands. It was alive, because several witnesses saw its tentacles moving in a convulsive way. But it is probable that it was dying. A gentleman named Pouchet obtained a rifle and shot it.

That was the last appearance of a living *Haploteuthis*. No others were seen on the French coast. On the 15th of June a dead carcass, almost complete, was washed ashore near Torquay, and a few days later a boat from the Marine Biological station, engaged in dredging off Plymouth, picked up a rotting specimen, slashed deeply with a cutlass wound. How the former had come by its death it is impossible to say. And on the last day of June, Mr. Egbert Caine, an artist, bathing near Newlyn, threw up his arms, shrieked, and was drawn under. A friend bathing with him made no attempt to save him, but swam at once for the shore. This is the last fact to tell of this extraordinary raid from the deeper sea. Whether it is really the last of these horrible creatures it is, as yet, premature to say. But it is believed, and certainly it is to be hoped, that they have returned now, and returned for good, to the sunless depths of the middle seas, out of which they have so strangely and so mysteriously arisen.

— The End —

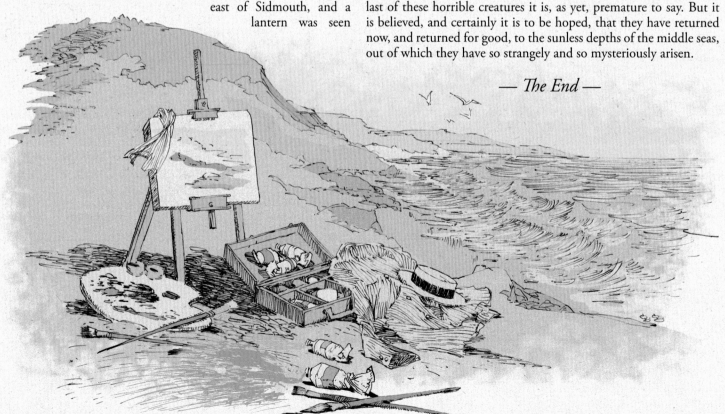

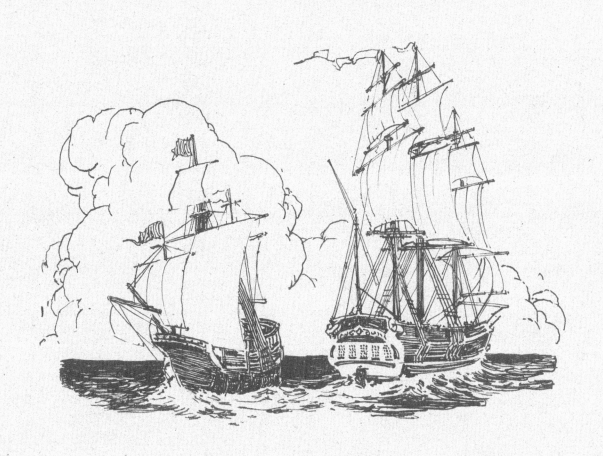

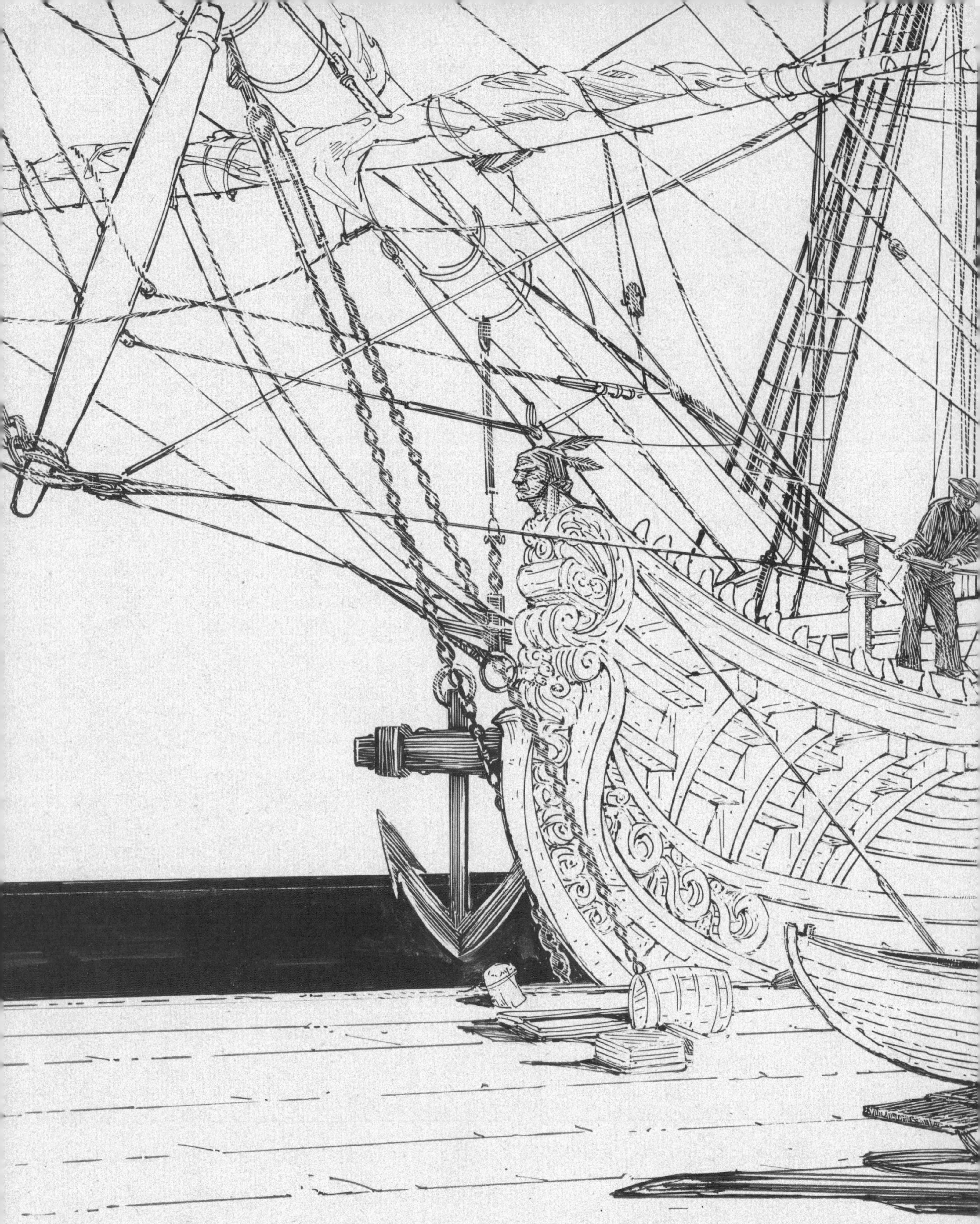